The Military History of World War II: Volume 12
THE NAVAL WAR IN THE PACIFIC
ON TO TOKYO

The Military History of World War II: Volume 12

THE NAVAL WAR
IN THE PACIFIC:
ON TO TOKYO

by Trevor Nevitt Dupuy
COL., U.S. ARMY, RET.

FRANKLIN WATTS, INC.
575 Lexington Avenue • New York 22

Maps by Dyno Lowenstein

Library of Congress Catalog Card Number: 62-7382
Copyright © 1963 by Franklin Watts, Inc.
Printed in the United States of America

1   2   3   4   5   6   7

Contents

Japanese marines charge through the ruins of Shanghai.

The Japanese Offensives

Outbreak of War

WORLD WAR II began in the Far East in the summer of 1937, when Japanese troops invaded China to begin what they called "the China Incident." This was the first move in the Japanese plan to establish political and economic control over all of East Asia, creating a "Greater East Asia Co-prosperity Sphere."

The outbreak of World War II in Europe seemed to give Japan the opportunity to proceed further. In 1940, Germany conquered Holland and France and decisively defeated British armies on the continent of Europe. None of these countries could offer serious opposition to Japan's ambitions in Southeast Asia. Moving into defenseless French Indochina, by the end of 1941 the Japanese had completed preparations for seizing British Malaya and the Netherlands East Indies. Japan ignored warnings from the United States that continued aggression could lead to war.

The Japanese were determined to seize the rich Southern Resources Area, even if this meant war with America. They felt sure that they could conquer these regions, as well as the American-held Philippine Islands, so quickly and so effectively that the American Navy and weak American Army would be unable to interfere.

The Japanese struck on December 7, 1941. In a devastating raid on the American naval base at Pearl Harbor, in Hawaii, they sank or seriously damaged all eight battleships of the American Pacific Fleet. At the same time Japanese naval, air, and land forces launched simultaneous attacks against all Western colonial possessions in the Far East and Southwest Pacific areas. In the first few days of the war, they seized British Hong Kong and American Wake and Guam islands.

1

Conquest of the Southern Resources Area

In Malaya, meanwhile, the Japanese navy supported army troops in an amazingly successful amphibious invasion. On December 10, 1941, swarms of Japanese naval aircraft based in Indochina attacked and sank the British battleship HMS *Prince of Wales* and the battle cruiser HMS *Repulse* off the coast of Malaya. In the following weeks, Japanese troops fought their way to the tip of the Malayan Peninsula, then across the Strait of Johore to attack the great British naval base at Singapore, which fell February 15.

Skillful defensive tactics on the parts of Generals Douglas MacArthur and Jonathan Wainwright stalled Japanese efforts to seize the isolated American strongholds of Bataan and Corregidor Island in the Philippines. Finally, however, in April and May, 1942, Japanese reinforcements and overwhelming combat power broke down the resistance of the starving American and Filipino troops.

The Japanese had, in the meantime, continued their planned offensive into the rich Netherlands East Indies. In January and February, 1942, strong amphibious forces leapfrogged southward through these islands toward the heart of the Dutch colonial empire on Java. An ill-assorted collection of American, Dutch, and British warships attempted to stop Japanese advances, but they were continually battered by Japanese airplanes, which dominated the skies. The larger, more modern, more powerful Japanese ships outfought them. On February 27, 1942, in the Battle of the Java Sea, the Allied naval squadron was decisively defeated by the Japanese. Most of the surviving Allied warships were hunted down and sunk in the waters around Java in the following days. By mid-March, the Netherlands East Indies were firmly in Japanese hands.

Soon after this, a powerful Japanese naval force sailed into the Indian Ocean to attack British air and naval bases in Ceylon and

2

India. It caused much damage, but also lost a number of planes to RAF fighters. By mid-April, when the Japanese carrier task force returned to the Pacific to rest and to rebuild the strength of its carrier air groups, Britain had been forced to abandon all of her naval bases in Ceylon and the central Indian Ocean.

Elsewhere, other Japanese land and naval forces were advancing southeastward into eastern New Guinea and the Solomon Islands. American, British, and Australian leaders feared that the Japanese might cut the sea and air routes from the United States to Australia and New Zealand before America could build up her fighting strength sufficiently to offer effective resistance.

Fortunately for the Allies, however, American code experts had broken the secret Japanese codes in the years before the war. So the Americans intercepted radio messages from Tokyo in April, 1942, ordering Japanese naval and land forces at Rabaul to seize Port Moresby in southeastern New Guinea. Admiral Chester W. Nimitz, then commanding American naval forces in the Pacific, at once sent Admiral Frank J. Fletcher with two aircraft carriers to the South Pacific to try to stop these Japanese thrusts.

Battles of the Coral Sea and of Midway

THE AMERICAN carriers — USS *Lexington* and USS *Yorktown* — accompanied by several cruisers and destroyers, sailed into the Coral Sea in early May, just as the Japanese invasion convoy started toward Port Moresby. The convoy was protected by two Japanese task forces, which included one light carrier and two heavy carriers.

The first carrier-against-carrier battle in history was fought on May 7 and 8, 1942. American planes sank the Japanese light carrier, and severely damaged one of the others. The Japanese hit both of

3

the American carriers, sinking the *Lexington*. Both sides then withdrew to avoid further punishment, so the battle was tactically a draw. However, with no air cover, the Japanese expedition to Port Moresby had to turn back. Thus the Americans accomplished their purpose, and the battle was a strategic American success. This was the first time a major naval battle had been fought without the exchange of a shot by surface ships.

Thinking that both the American carriers had been sunk, and knowing that the carrier USS *Hornet* had arrived in that part of the Pacific too late to take part in the battle, Admiral Isoroku Yamamoto, who commanded the Japanese Combined Fleet, decided that the time was ripe for a swift attack on the American island of Midway. This island would provide the Japanese with a splendid advanced outpost in the Central Pacific.

Late in May, Yamamoto advanced against Midway with a great armada consisting of four heavy and two light aircraft carriers, eleven battleships, and many other warships. In addition. his fleet was accompanied by transports carrying five thousand soldiers prepared to occupy Midway. At the same time, two Japanese light carriers and other warships made a diversionary raid against the Aleutian Islands.

Because the Americans were still reading the Japanese coded radio messages, Admiral Nimitz soon learned of Yamamoto's plan. He could assemble only three aircraft carriers and some cruisers and destroyers to meet the powerful Japanese fleet, but as his ships waited for the Japanese near Midway, he had the advantage of surprise.

On June 4, 1942, Japanese carrier-based aircraft delivered a heavy blow against Midway, then drove off American planes from Midway that were attempting to strike back at the carriers. Later in the day, however, in an exchange of carrier strikes, the American planes sank

4

An American aircraft carrier sinks during the Battle of the Coral Seas.

all four Japanese heavy cruisers. The American carrier USS *Yorktown* was severely damaged by Japanese carrier planes, and two days later was sunk by Japanese submarines. This was really a small price for the Americans to pay, however, for they had wiped out the most important striking element of the Japanese fleet. Admiral Yamamoto, now forced to give up his plan to capture Midway, ordered a retreat.

The Battle of Midway was the turning point of the Pacific war. Japanese planes and warships could no longer dominate the oceans. The only thing the Japanese had accomplished was the seizure of the tiny, uninhabited islands of Attu and Kiska in the Aleutians.

During the Battle of Midway, as in the Battle of the Coral Sea, surface vessels of the opposing sides never saw one another.

Japanese midget submarine, scuttled by her two-man crew during the naval Battle of Guadalcanal, November, 1942, and later raised by American Seabees. Nearby is the rotting hulk of a Japanese transport.

The Struggle for Guadalcanal

THE AMERICAN Joint Chiefs of Staff now decided to attack Japanese outposts in the southern Solomon Islands. On August 7, 1942, the 1st Marine Division landed on Guadalcanal and Tulagi. On Guadalcanal the Marines seized a partly completed Japanese airfield, which they renamed Henderson Field. This was the beginning of six months of bitter fighting on Guadalcanal, and on the sea and in the air nearby.

The American fleet lost a few more ships than the Japanese in the fierce surface engagements around Guadalcanal. But during this same period, American land-based and carrier-based airplanes gained control of the air over the southern Solomon Islands. Because of this, and because of the Marines' grim defense of vital Henderson Field, American planes were able to punish the Japanese naval squadrons and reinforcement convoys so severely that the losses

This photograph of a Japanese troopship under assault by American planes graphically illustrates the role of air power in the Pacific naval war. The crewmen of the ship are trying vainly to lower a lifeboat over the side of the crippled ship.

U.S. AIR FORCE PHOTO

finally became heavier than the Japanese could afford. In early February, 1942, in one last, daring exploit, Japanese destroyers came down secretly from Rabaul to evacuate the starving survivors of the Japanese garrison.

Meanwhile, in Papua (eastern New Guinea), General MacArthur's troops had repulsed an overland Japanese offensive against Port Moresby. The Allies had then recaptured bases that the Japanese had seized at Buna and Gona, on the northeastern coast of Papua.

The Japanese now realized that their offensives against the Allies would have to be called off. They still felt confident, however, that the defensive part of their war plan would work out successfully. They believed that American attacks against their chain of island bases would be so costly that the United States would soon be willing to make peace.

7

THE GLOBAL SITUATION AT THE BEGINNING OF 1943

FINLAND

● **MOSCOW**

● Stalingrad

GERMANY

SPAIN

TURKEY

MOROCCO

TUNISIA

● El Alamein

ALGERIA

LIBYA

EGYPT

IND

FRENCH WEST AFRICA

EQUATOR

AXIS-CONTROLLED,
JANUARY , 1943

U.S.S.R.

ALASKA

Komandorski Is.

Attu • Kiska

International
Date Line

OUTER MONGOLIA

MANCHUKUO

KOREA

CHINA

TOKYO

Midway I.

Formosa

JAPAN

HAWAIIAN IS.

BURMA

THAILAND

FR. INDOCHINA

PHILIPPINE ISL.

Wake Is.

• Guam

EQUATOR

PAPUA

Guadalcanal

AUSTRALIA

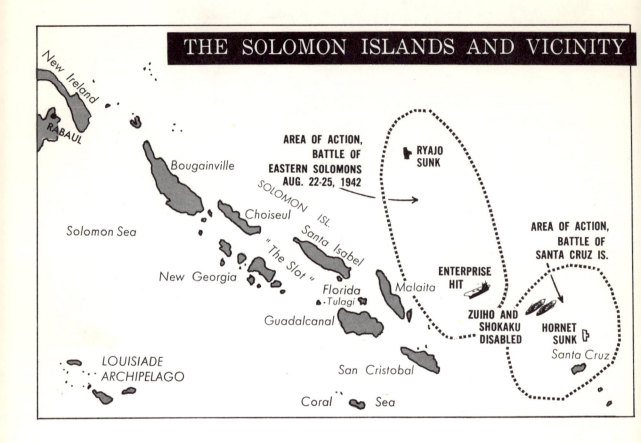

THE SOLOMON ISLANDS AND VICINITY

New Ireland

RABAUL

Bougainville

Choiseul

Solomon Sea

New Georgia

"The Slot"

Santa Isabel

SOLOMON ISL.

Florida
• Tulagi

Guadalcanal

Malaita

San Cristobal

LOUISIADE
ARCHIPELAGO

Coral   Sea

AREA OF ACTION,
BATTLE OF
EASTERN SOLOMONS
AUG. 22-25, 1942

RYAJO
SUNK

ENTERPRISE
HIT

ZUIHO AND
SHOKAKU
DISABLED

AREA OF ACTION,
BATTLE OF
SANTA CRUZ IS.

HORNET
SUNK

Santa Cruz

Through the Solomons Toward Rabaul

Allied Strategy and the New Allied Team

THE BRITISH-AMERICAN Combined Chiefs of Staff had agreed that the first and most important Allied task in the war should be the defeat of Germany. But by early 1943 American industry was producing many more warships than were needed for either the closing phase of the Battle of the Atlantic or the support of Allied landing operations in the Mediterranean and Normandy. Most of these ships were sent to join the growing American fleets in the Pacific.

Ground and air reinforcements were also sent to General MacArthur's Southwest Pacific Theater and to Admiral Nimitz' Pacific Ocean Areas. From his base on Oahu, Admiral Nimitz was responsible for a predominantly naval offensive through Japan's Central Pacific islands. At the same time, General MacArthur was to conduct a drive northward in eastern New Guinea toward Rabaul, on New Britain, and then to turn northwestward toward the Philippines.

American Navy, Army, and Marine forces in and around Guadalcanal had been under the control of Admiral Nimitz. Now designated the Third Fleet, and commanded by Vice Admiral William F. Halsey, these forces were temporarily placed under MacArthur to assist in the advance toward Rabaul.

The Death of Yamamoto

MEANWHILE, Admiral Yamamoto, trying to strengthen the southeastern corner of the Japanese defense perimeter, realized that he could not hold Rabaul or the Solomons without immediately strengthening the air units based at Rabaul. He did this by taking more than two hundred planes from his main carrier force at Truk. He expected to replace these planes and pilots with new carrier groups that were then receiving intensive training in Japan.

In April, 1943, Yamamoto began an inspection tour of the forward outposts of his perimeter. Having again broken the Japanese code, the Americans were still reading Japanese radio messages, and so they learned of the admiral's planned trip. As Yamamoto arrived by air and attempted to make a landing at Bougainville, a waiting squadron of Army Air Force fighters shot down his plane in flames. Yamamoto's death was a severe blow to the Japanese. On April 21, Admiral Mineichi Koga was appointed the new commander of the Combined Fleet.

Night Battles in the Solomons

BY JUNE, 1943, Halsey had received enough reinforcements to begin his offensive in the Solomons. On June 30, the Third Amphibious Force, commanded by Rear Admiral R. K. Turner, supported a Marine-Army landing on Rendova Island. This was followed two days later by landings near Munda, on neighboring New Georgia Island. As they had done in the Guadalcanal campaign, the Japanese sent reinforcements by fast destroyer to their embattled troops.

This led to three small but sharp naval night actions in the central Solomons during July and August. Japanese night-fighting skill overcame American radar and superior numbers to win the Battles of Kula Gulf, July 5-6, and, a week later, of Kolombangara. Several Allied cruisers and destroyers were lost to deadly Japanese torpedoes. During the night of August 6-7, however, six American destroyers partly evened the score by sinking three out of four Japanese destroyers in the Battle of Vella Gulf.

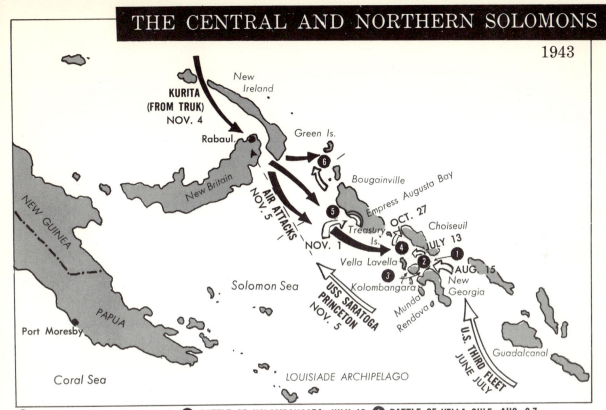

① BATTLE OF KULA GULF, JULY 6 **②** BATTLE OF KOLOMBANGARA, JULY 13 **③** BATTLE OF VELLA GULF, AUG. 6-7
④ BATTLE OF VELLA LAVELLA, OCT. 6-7 **⑤** BATTLE OF EMPRESS AUGUSTA BAY, NOV. 2 **⑥** BATTLE OF CAPE ST. GEORGE, NOV. 25

On August 15, the Third Amphibious Force, now commanded by
Rear Admiral Theodore S. Wilkinson, began landings of soldiers and
Marines on Vella Lavella, bypassing more heavily defended Kolombangara Island. In September the Japanese successfully evacuated
their ten thousand men from Kolombangara, despite American efforts to intercept them.

During the first week of October, the Japanese began to evacuate
the survivors of their troops still fighting on Vella Lavella. On the
night of October 6-7, three American destroyers discovered six Japanese destroyers and a number of smaller craft approaching Vella
Lavella.

13

Again the advantage of radar permitted the Americans to open the battle by sinking a Japanese destroyer, but again the Japanese fought back with torpedoes. They sank one of the American destroyers and damaged both of the others. Then, as additional American destroyers approached the scene of action, the Japanese withdrew. Meanwhile, the Japanese small craft had quickly evacuated the waiting Japanese soldiers. This Battle of Vella Lavella, however, was to be the last clear-cut Japanese naval victory over the Americans.

Admiral Halsey's next objective was to establish a base on the west coast of Bougainville. As a diversion, small landings were made on October 27 on the Treasury Islands and on Choiseul. Then, on November 1, the Third Amphibious Force, supported by a carrier group from the Central Pacific Fleet, put fourteen thousand Marines and soldiers ashore at Empress Augusta Bay.

A Japanese squadron of four cruisers and six destroyers, commanded by Rear Admiral Sentaro Omori, dashed down from Rabaul. But Rear Admiral A. Stanton Merrill's Task Force 39 — four light cruisers and eight destroyers — was waiting off Empress Augusta Bay. Making excellent use of their radar, the Americans attacked Omori's force from front and flanks. Though the Japanese were assisted by flares dropped from supporting aircraft, they lost a cruiser and a destroyer. With most of his remaining ships damaged, Omori withdrew. The Americans had one destroyer badly damaged.

Admiral Koga then sent Vice Admiral Takeo Kurita, with a cruiser and destroyer force from Truk, to attack the American beachhead on Bougainville. While refueling at Rabaul, on November 5, Kurita's squadron was struck by planes from the USS *Saratoga* and USS *Princeton*. Six Japanese cruisers and two destroyers were badly damaged; Kurita had to abandon his planned attack.

In the early morning darkness of November 25, a squadron of five

Aircraft carrier USS Saratoga.

destroyers under Captain Arleigh Burke intercepted five Japanese destroyers southeast of New Ireland. In the Battle of Cape Saint George, the Americans sank three of the Japanese vessels without suffering serious damage themselves.

Decline of the Japanese Naval Air Force

WHILE these surface battles were taking place in the Solomons, a more decisive struggle was raging in the air. America, with her great airplane construction program, combined with a highly efficient pilot training system, was producing trained air units more rapidly than Japan could. This, combined with the series of naval air losses that had begun at Midway, had put the Japanese at a serious disad-

15

Flying under the guns of Japanese defenses, Fifth Air Force B-25 low level attacking bombers have just swept Rabaul Harbor. Four enemy ships are left burning and sinking, one a 1,000 ton cruiser. In this one raid, 114,000 tons of shipping were destroyed.

vantage in the continuing air fighting over the Solomons. On top of this, American long-range, land-based bombers from Henderson Field and from bases in New Guinea were inflicting terrible losses on the main Japanese air bases in and around Rabaul.

In a few months, the carrier air groups which Yamamoto had sent to Rabaul from Truk had been almost wiped out. Replacement pilots were not so well trained as their predecessors had been. As pilot experience and ability declined, Japanese losses mounted, and this led to more replacements with still less experience and ability. Because of this vicious cycle, Japanese air losses became staggering. By the end of 1943, Japan had lost almost three thousand planes and pilots in the Solomons air struggle alone.

16

General MacArthur's Navy

The Seventh Fleet

EARLY IN 1943, the small American and Australian naval forces in General MacArthur's Southwest Pacific Ocean Area were reorganized as the Seventh Fleet, under the command first of Vice Admiral A. S. Carpender, and later of Vice Admiral Thomas C. Kinkaid. The principal task of this fleet was to gain and keep control of the coastal waters of New Guinea and to support MacArthur's ground troops in their numerous amphibious landings along that coast.

The actual conduct of these amphibious landings was entrusted to the Seventh Amphibious Force — a collection of gunfire support warships, specialized amphibious vessels and landing craft, as well as highly trained Army engineers and Navy Seabees whose task was to clear beach obstacles and to organize beachhead administration and supply. Commanding this efficient, smoothly functioning team of ships and men was Rear Admiral Daniel E. Barbey.

Battle of the Bismarck Sea

JUST BEFORE the Seventh Fleet was established, an important engagement took place between General MacArthur's forces and Japanese warships in the Bismarck Sea. The only Allied units engaged were Australian and American aircraft of General George C. Kenney's Fifth Air Force.

On February 28, 1943, a Japanese convoy of eight small merchant vessels, carrying more than seven thousand troops and escorted by eight destroyers, sailed from Rabaul to reinforce Lae, the principal Japanese stronghold in Papua. On March 2, despite stormy, foggy weather, Allied medium bombers attacked the convoy.

17

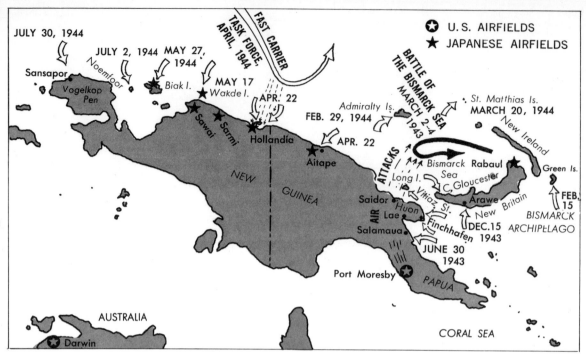

NORTHERN NEW GUINEA AND THE BISMARCK ARCHIPELAGO 1943-1944

The battle raged for three days, as the Allied planes surprised the Japanese by coming in under the clouds to make low-level skip-bombing attacks. The battle ended on March 4, when Allied planes sank the last Japanese troop transport. Only four of the Japanese destroyers survived. These returned to Rabaul, badly damaged.

Amphibious Operations in Papua and New Britain

IN JUNE, 1943, at about the same time that Admiral Halsey began his advance in the Solomons, General MacArthur started his offensive. Units of General Walter Krueger's Sixth Army landed south of Salamaua in the first of many amphibious leaps along the New Guinea shore. The efficient Seventh Fleet and Seventh Amphibious Force

18

next supported landings east of Lae in the Huon Gulf early in September, then later that same month, just north of Finschhafen, at the eastern extremity of the Huon Peninsula. In December, several more landings were made on the north shore of Vitiaz Strait on Long Island, and between Arawe and Cape Gloucester in southwestern New Britain.

In the early months of 1944, the tempo increased. The Seventh Fleet provided magnificent support in landings at Saidor in January; in the Admiralty Islands in February; and in the St. Matthias Islands in March. Meanwhile, in February, Halsey's Third Amphibious Force placed New Zealand troops on the Green Islands between Bougainville and Rabaul.

The great Japanese base of Rabaul, with nearly 100,000 men, was now almost surrounded, and was practically isolated by American air and naval action. Since these troops were no longer able to interfere with his advance, MacArthur bypassed Rabaul.

ARMY AIR FORCE PHOTO

The ship-packed circular harbor at Rabaul, New Britain Island, was a prime target for incoming American flyers. The harbor was a main Japanese stronghold.

High moment of attack on a Japanese air base near Wewak, in northeastern New Guinea. Twenty Japanese aircraft were set afire, twenty more seriously damaged.

Along the New Guinea Coast

MacArthur now turned northwest along the coast of New Guinea. His next objective was Hollandia. This was beyond the operational range of his land-based fighter planes in northeastern New Guinea, so the Japanese were sure he would not attack it. But MacArthur obtained naval air assistance from Admiral Nimitz' Pacific Ocean Areas.

Nimitz sent his powerful Fast Carrier Task Force. At the end of March, 1943, the carrier planes struck the Palau Islands and Yap in order to neutralize the Japanese air bases north of New Guinea.

20

B-25 (upper right) slips down on a group of Japanese coastal vessels off New Guinea.

Then the carriers swept back to the waters north of Hollandia. While carrier planes blasted beaches and nearby Japanese airfields, the Seventh Fleet and the Seventh Amphibious Force landed American troops at Hollandia and Aitape.

The Japanese were completely surprised. Opposition was negligible; a great victory was won in seemingly uneventful, routine operations. Again the Japanese perimeter was broken.

As his troops continued westward along the northern coast of New Guinea, MacArthur continued to receive the same kind of superb naval support in landings which eventually gave the Allies complete control of the northern coast of New Guinea.

21

Leapfrog Across the Pacific

Operations in the North Pacific

DURING LATE 1942 and early 1943 the Japanese footholds in the Aleutian Islands at Kiska and Attu were frequently bombarded from the sea and the air. These attacks, combined with American air and naval patrol of the waters between Kiska and the Kuriles, made it very difficult for the Japanese to maintain a naval supply line to these outposts.

Accordingly, in early March of 1943, Vice Admiral Boshiro Hosogaya began to escort supply ships to the Japanese Aleutian outposts with a strong carrier-destroyer force. After one successful supply run, Hosogaya's second trip was intercepted just south of the Komandorskie Islands at dawn on March 27 by an American task group under Rear Admiral Charles H. McMorris. The Japanese squadron consisted of two heavy cruisers, two light cruisers, six destroyers, and two transports. McMorris had a heavy cruiser, a light cruiser, and four destroyers.

In a three-hour battle, the heavy cruiser *Salt Lake City* was completely disabled, and McMorris' destroyers were also badly damaged. But though the Japanese vessels had suffered less punishment, Hosogaya did not follow up his advantage. Realizing that American land-based planes were on the way, he broke off the action and returned to the Kuriles. The Japanese made no further efforts to reinforce Kiska and Attu by surface ship. Henceforward they relied only upon submarines.

In May, an amphibious force commanded by Rear Admiral Thomas C. Kinkaid landed on Attu, and captured it after a tough fight. On July 28, a Japanese cruiser and destroyer squadron skill-

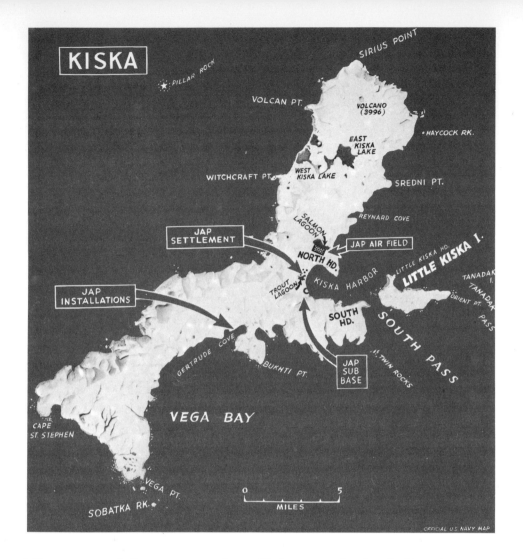

KISKA

PILLAR ROCK

SIRIUS POINT

VOLCAN PT.

VOLCANO
(3996)

HAYCOCK RK.

EAST
KISKA
LAKE

WITCHCRAFT PT.

WEST
KISKA LAKE

SREDNI PT.

SALMON
LAGOON

REYNARD COVE

JAP
SETTLEMENT

NORTH HD.

JAP AIR FIELD

LITTLE KISKA HD.

LITTLE KISKA I.

TANADAK
I.

KISKA HARBOR

TANADAK
ORIENT PT.

PASS

JAP
INSTALLATIONS

TROUT
LAGOON

SOUTH
HD.

SOUTH PASS

GERTRUDE COVE

BUKHTI PT.

JAP
SUB
BASE

TWIN ROCKS

VEGA BAY

CAPE
ST. STEPHEN

VEGA PT.

0   5
MILES

SOBATKA RK.

OFFICIAL U.S. NAVY MAP

fully evacuated their garrison from Kiska, completely eluding American air and naval patrols. Not realizing that the Japanese had left, Kinkaid's amphibious force assaulted Kiska, after a heavy air and naval bombardment The Americans were embarrassed to discover that they had been shooting at a nonexistent foe. But the Japanese had been driven from their only footholds in the Western Hemisphere.

23

Preparations in the Central Pacific

MEANWHILE, Admiral Nimitz — Supreme Commander of the Pacific Ocean Areas and also Commander in Chief of the Pacific Fleet — was preparing for the principal American naval offensive. His growing fleet was built around the Fast Carrier Task Force, which, by the fall of 1943, consisted of twelve carriers and nearly eight hundred aircraft. These and other combat elements of the fleet were commanded directly by brilliant, austere Rear Admiral Raymond A. Spruance, who had returned from the Battle of Midway, just a year earlier, with only two carriers. Later, Nimitz combined these forces into the Fifth Fleet, which Spruance commanded until the end of the war.

To convoy and support his Army and Marine assault troops in their coming landing operations on Central Pacific islands, Admiral Nimitz established the Fifth Amphibious Force at Pearl Harbor in the summer of 1943. Rear Admiral R. K. Turner was brought from the Solomons to organize and command this force.

Invading the Gilberts

BY THE FALL of 1943, Nimitz' forces were ready to begin the offensive. The first important amphibious operation in the Central Pacific took place on the beaches of the Gilbert Islands at Makin and Tarawa on November 21, 1943. (This was November 20 in Hawaii and the United States.) While Turner's Amphibious Force was approaching, the Fast Carrier Task Force struck not only at the Gilberts, but at all nearby Japanese island strongholds.

Although the Navy pounded the beaches of Tarawa with a heavy preassault carrier air and naval gun bombardment, the attacking Marines ran into unexpectedly fierce and determined opposition. Resistance was much less intense on Makin, where troops of the

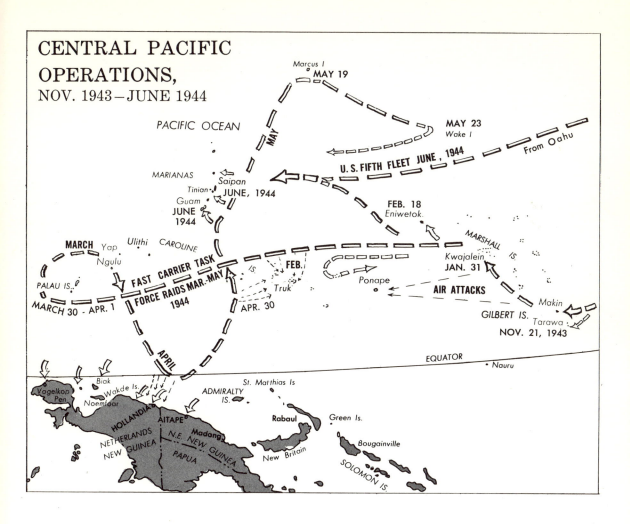

CENTRAL PACIFIC OPERATIONS,
NOV. 1943 – JUNE 1944

PACIFIC OCEAN

Marcus I
MAY 19

MAY 23
Wake I

From Oahu

U.S. FIFTH FLEET JUNE, 1944

MAY

MARIANAS
Saipan
Tinian
JUNE, 1944
Guam
JUNE
1944

FEB. 18
Eniwetok

MARSHALL IS.

Kwajalein
JAN. 31

MARCH
Yap
Ngulu
Ulithi
CAROLINE

FAST CARRIER TASK
FORCE RAIDS MAR.-MAY
1944

PALAU IS.

MARCH 30 - APR. 1

FEB.

Truk

APR. 30

Ponape

AIR ATTACKS

Makin

GILBERT IS.
Tarawa
NOV. 21, 1943

APRIL

EQUATOR
Nauru

Vogelkop
Pen.
Biak
Wakde Is.
Noemfoor
HOLLANDIA
AITAPE
NETHERLANDS
NEW GUINEA
PAPUA
Madang
N.E. NEW GUINEA

St. Matthias Is.
ADMIRALTY
IS.

Rabaul

Green Is.

New Britain

Bougainville

SOLOMON IS.

Marines take cover behind sea wall on Tarawa.

Army's 27th Division landed. Both islands were finally secure, however, by November 24.

Tarawa provided a number of lessons, not only to the troops making the landings, but to the Navy that was supporting them. New techniques were designed for preassault bombardment and for the gunfire support of troops once they were ashore. The Marines paid a heavy price in casualties for the capture of Tarawa, but the lessons learned in this relatively small operation saved many thousands of lives in later operations.

Command and Administration in the Central Pacific

BY THE BEGINNING of 1944, Admiral Nimitz was well satisfied with his team of commanders and his major operating forces. The latest member was Rear Admiral Marc A. Mitscher who, in January, 1944, joined Spruance's Fifth Fleet as the commander of the growing Fast Carrier Task Force, now designated as Task Force 58.

The Central Pacific assault force of Marines and soldiers was designated as the V Marine Amphibious Corps, commanded by hard-bitten, crusty Major General Howland M. Smith — known to his fellow Marines as "Howling Mad" Smith. He became an indispensable member of the team of Nimitz, Spruance, Mitscher, Turner, and Smith.

Nimitz and his staff realized that in order to carry the war into the Japanese-dominated waters of the Western Pacific, the fleet would have to be able to stay at sea for long periods of time, to fight, and to protect the assault troops once they had landed. Therefore the ships would need to be resupplied with fuel, ammunition, and food, and would have to receive replacements for sick and wounded men. So the Pacific Fleet had developed a system for resupplying the ships of the fleet at sea, even during battle. This was done by the Logistic Support Group and by its "sea trains" of fast cargo ships and tankers, which became moving bases for the fleet.

Carrying fuel oil, gasoline, ammunition, and other needed supplies, these trains would sail at regular intervals from bases like Pearl Harbor to meet and to supply the fleet at sea. The fast cargo ships would steam up beside the warships at full speed. None of the vessels could slow down, because of possible torpedo attacks from lurking Japanese submarines. Rope lines would be thrown across the narrow strip of water between the two speeding ships, then oil hoses and cargo chutes would be rigged between them.

It was not uncommon for a tanker to be steaming at full speed between a carrier and a destroyer, pumping fuel oil into each of them, while another cargo vessel would be on the other side of the carrier, delivering ammunition, food, and mail through cargo chutes, and sending men swinging above the leaping waves in breeches buoys. As soon as one warship was resupplied, the cargo vessel would move on to the next. In this way the fleet could be refueled and resupplied in a few hours.

Invasion of the Marshalls

AFTER the seizure of the Gilbert Islands, Admiral Nimitz decided to bypass the easternmost Japanese outposts and to strike at Kwajalein Atoll, in the heart of the Marshalls. During the last week of January, the groups of Mitscher's Fast Carrier Task Force neutralized the bypassed bases, as well as Eniwetok, in the northwestern Marshalls.

As a result of the lessons learned at Tarawa, the islands of Kwajalein were given a far more intensive preassault bombardment. This was carried out by Army Air Force land-based planes operating from new airfields established in the Gilberts, as well as by the carrier aircraft and by naval gunfire. As a result, when the Marine and Army troops went ashore on February 1 and 2, they encountered less resistance near the beaches than they had met at Tarawa. By February 8, the principal islands of the atoll were secured.

The American seizure of Kwajalein exposed the main Japanese naval base at Truk to naval and air attack, and so Admiral Koga decided to withdraw his Combined Fleet to the Palaus and to Singapore.

Admiral Spruance, meanwhile, had turned his attention toward Eniwetok. To neutralize nearby Japanese airfields, Army Air Force planes from the Gilberts hammered at Ponape, and most of the Fifth Fleet struck a series of powerful blows at Truk on February 17 and 18. In this furious American air and surface attack, the Japanese lost about two hundred aircraft, ten naval vessels, and twenty-nine mer-

A typical sight over the Pacific was the Navy scout plane flying above troop-laden landing craft headed for the beaches.

U.S. NAVY DEPARTMENT

chant ships. One American carrier was damaged by a Japanese torpedo plane, and twenty-five American flyers were shot down during the two-day battle.

On February 18, while Truk was being so badly battered, a small American amphibious force assaulted Eniwetok. As at Kwajalein, intensive preassault bombardment helped the Marines get ashore without too much interference. Although Japanese resistance was stronger further inland, the Marines captured the island by February 22.

Raids of the Fast Carrier Task Force

FROM MARCH through June, Mitscher's carriers, supported by Army planes based on the newly captured islands kept up continuous air pressure against Japanese strongholds in the Marianas, the western Carolines, and the Palaus. All of these air attacks were closely coordinated with operations of the Far Eastern Air Forces of the Southwest Pacific Command, whose planes were also raiding in the southern Carolines.

The most intensive of the carrier strikes was a great raid on the Palaus, between March 30 and April 1. It was carried out by planes from 11 carriers. In three days these planes destroyed 150 Japanese planes and 100,000 tons of naval and merchant shipping. They also blockaded the harbor entrances with mines, and at the same time they severely damaged air and naval installations. American losses were 25 planes.

Thinking this was the beginning of a major American attack, on March 31 Admiral Koga flew away from the battered Palaus to establish a new headquarters at Davao, on the Philippine island of Mindanao. His plane got lost in the fog and crashed, killing all on

A 40-mm gun crew opens fire as Japanese planes approach.

board. Japan had lost its second Combined Fleet commander in less than a year.

A month later, Task Force 58 carried out another intensive attack on Truk. Ninety Japanese planes were destroyed in the air or on the ground, against a loss of twenty-seven American planes. On May 19 and 23, the carriers attacked the Japanese island outposts of Marcus and Wake Islands.

The war was coming close to Japan.

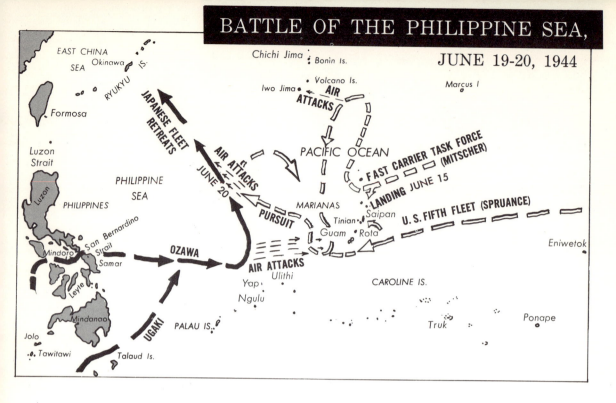

Battle of the Philippine Sea

Invasion of the Marianas

ON MAY 3, Japanese Imperial Headquarters appointed Admiral Soemu Toyoda as commander of the Combined Fleet. To be near the oilfields of Tarakan, in Borneo, Toyoda sent Admiral Jisaburo Ozawa's First Mobile Fleet, organized around nine carriers, to the island anchorage of Tawitawi, between the Philippines and Borneo. Here the depleted carrier air groups were built up to full strength by the arrival of newly trained and relatively inexperienced pilots from Japan.

Early in June, Toyoda ordered most of the surface force of the Mobile Fleet to assist the defenders of Biak against General Mac-

32

Arthur's latest advance. He hoped to strike a damaging blow at the Seventh Fleet and to isolate the American beachhead. But this force, under Vice Admiral Matome Ugaki, had barely started toward Biak when Toyoda learned that a tremendous American armada was sailing from the Marshall Islands toward the Marianas. Calling back Ugaki, he ordered Ozawa to strike with all of the Mobile Fleet against the new threat.

This was Admiral Spruance's Fifth Fleet, which had sailed from the Marshalls on June 6, closely followed by more than 500 vessels of Admiral Turner's Fifth Amphibious Force, carrying 130,000 troops to assault the Marianas. On June 11, the planes of Task Force 58 struck the Marianas, where they encountered relatively slight resistance in the air. Most of the Japanese planes there had been sent down to help in the defense of Biak.

The surface bombardment of Saipan and Tinian began on June 13. Half of Mitscher's planes continued to pound the Marianas, while the remainder of Task Force 58 steamed north to strike Japanese airfields on Iwo Jima and Chichi Jima. This made it difficult for the Japanese to send air reinforcements to the Marianas from Japan.

The landing on Saipan began on June 15. Against stronger opposition than had been expected, the Marines and soldiers began to battle their way inland from the beaches.

Approach of the Japanese Fleet

THE MORNING after the Saipan landings, Admiral Spruance received a submarine report that Ozawa's fleet was approaching from the west. Spruance called off a planned landing on Guam, scheduled for June 18. He had some of the troops intended for the Guam landing put ashore on Saipan, and sent the rest eastward, so as to be out of the way of the coming naval battle.

Ozawa's fleet consisted of 9 carriers, 5 battleships, 13 cruisers and 28 destroyers. There were 473 planes on the carriers. Spruance sailed westward of the Marianas with 15 carriers carrying 956 planes, 7 battleships, 21 cruisers, and 69 destroyers.

Although the Japanese fleet was outnumbered, Ozawa had two important advantages — and thought he had a third. His light and maneuverable fighter planes could fly nearly 700 miles with a full load of gasoline and ammunition. This gave them a round-trip range of over 300 miles, while the heavier American aircraft had a range of only slightly more than 200 miles. In addition, the prevailing easterly winds in the Philippine Sea would permit the Japanese to launch and recover their planes while sailing eastward toward the Americans. Mitscher's carriers, on the other hand, would have to reverse course, to eastward, every time their planes took off or landed. This would delay the ships and would still further reduce the effective range of the American planes. Finally, Ozawa was counting on having his effective air strength doubled by nearly 500 land-based planes on the nearby airfields of Rota, Guam, and Yap.

Ozawa rightly believed that, in order to maintain constant protection of the amphibious force and the troops ashore, Spruance would not move beyond air range of the Saipan beachhead. The Japanese admiral, therefore, planned to launch his strike planes while his ships were beyond effective reach of the American aircraft.

After making their strike against Task Force 58, the Japanese carrier groups would land on Guam to reload fuel and ammunition. They would then take off, attacking the American fleet again on the way back to their carriers. All this while Ozawa felt that he could keep most of his fleet between three hundred and four hundred miles from the American carriers, and safely out of range of their planes.

34

Spruance guessed the Japanese battle plan, but felt he had no choice but to accept battle on Ozawa's terms, counting on the superior skill and numbers of the American carrier groups. The American admiral feared that if he ventured too far west of the Marianas, part of the Japanese fleet could circle around the flanks of Task Force 58 to strike the Saipan beachhead and convoys offshore.

On the afternoon of June 18, when Spruance realized that he could not hit the Japanese that day, he turned his fleet eastward, toward the islands. At dawn next morning the Americans were less than 100 miles from Guam, and about 350 miles east of the Japanese Mobile Fleet. Just as Ozawa had hoped, the American fleet was between his carriers and Japanese airfields in the Marianas, and within range of both.

"The Marianas Turkey Shoot"

THE JAPANESE FLEET was divided into two main groups. The van, commanded by Vice Admiral Kurita, had three light carriers and most of the heavy surface vessels. Almost one hundred miles farther southwest was Ozawa's main body: five heavy carriers, one light carrier, and several screening cruisers and destroyers.

Shortly after dawn on June 19, the Japanese carriers began to send their planes on their strike missions against Task Force 58. Ozawa was counting on an early attack by land-based planes from Guam and Rota to keep the Americans confused and busy, and to reduce their aircraft striking strength. But because of the American strikes against the Marianas and Bonin bases in previous days, there were only thirty-eight operational Japanese planes in the Marianas that morning. As these took off to attack the American ships, they themselves were struck, just after takeoff, or on the ground, by Mitscher's alert planes, already waiting in the air above them.

Beginning at 10:00 in the morning, the Japanese carrier planes began their attacks against the American fleet. But either because of Ozawa's error, or because of the poor state of training of the Japanese pilots, the attacks came in widely separated waves and with little coordination between waves.

American F6F Hellcat fighter planes were waiting, high in the air above the fleet. As the Japanese planes approached, the American fighters dove down upon them in devastating coordinated attacks. Meanwhile, Mitscher's bombers were hammering the Guam and Rota airfields to make them unusable.

Over a period of eight hours, four successive waves of Japanese planes flew in from the southwest, in groups averaging about one hundred each. Each wave suffered the same fate. Only about forty of the Japanese aircraft got through the defensive fighters, and half

Nakajima "Jill," a three-seater Japanese navy bomber that first came into combat around 1944 at Bougainville. Many of these high-speed Japanese craft were destroyed in the "Turkey Shoot."

F6F "Hellcat" fighter.

of these were shot down by the ships' curtain of intensive antiaircraft fire. Bomb hits caused slight damage to the battleships USS *South Dakota* and USS *Indiana,* but no American warships suffered any loss in fighting efficiency.

About 370 Japanese planes were shot down during this spectacular aerial battle, which the American flyers called the "Marianas Turkey Shoot." Counting the land-based planes destroyed in the early morning, total Japanese losses were more than 400 aircraft. Twenty-six American planes were lost; but about half of their pilots were saved.

Meanwhile, the main body of Ozawa's fleet had been attacked by the American submarines *Albacore* and *Cavalla.* The heavy carriers *Taiho* and *Shokaku* were sunk by torpedoes. Admiral Ozawa was rescued from his flagship, the *Taiho,* and transferred to the carrier *Zuikaku.* By nightfall, when he learned that he had only one hundred planes left, he decided to withdraw.

"Turn on the Lights"

NOW SPRUANCE felt that he could carry the fight directly to the Japanese fleet. Leaving one carrier group to cover the Saipan beachhead, Spruance steamed westward at full speed during the night with the remainder of Task Force 58. Next morning — June 20 — American patrol planes searched unsuccessfully for the Japanese fleet, which was now heading northwestward, toward the Ryukyus. Not until afternoon did an American patrol plane sight the Mobile Fleet more than 250 miles away. Although this was beyond the theoretical attack range of the American planes, and although it was late in the afternoon, Mitscher decided to strike, and turned east to launch his planes.

Within half an hour of receiving word of the location of the Japanese fleet, 216 planes — a full deckload from each carrier — were in the air, and Mitscher had turned his carriers back to a northwesterly course, racing after his planes as fast as his ships could steam. Every mile might mean the difference of life or death to many of those pilots, for they would be running out of gas as they returned to the carriers.

At about 6:00 P.M., the American planes reached the fleeing Japanese fleet. Ozawa sent seventy-five of his planes into the air to try to intercept the Americans. Ten of the attacking planes were shot down, but in turn the Americans destroyed forty of the Japanese planes. Then, braving intense antiaircraft fire, the American bomber and torpedo planes struck the carriers. In a few minutes they sank one heavy carrier and two oil tankers, while severely damaging two more heavy carriers, two light carriers, a battleship, a heavy cruiser, and another oiler. Ten more American planes were shot down. Then, with gas tanks dangerously low, and with night descending over the ocean, the 196 surviving American planes turned eastward.

38

While the planes were returning, Mitscher debated whether he should turn on the carrier lights to guide his pilots in. He realized that this would not only risk the lives of many more men, but would also expose his valuable ships to possible attacks from Japanese submarines. Yet he felt that he could not order his pilots to undertake such a dangerous mission without letting them know that the rest of the fleet was also willing to take risks. Quietly he issued the order, "Turn on the lights!"

The carriers' lights blazed on at once. At the same time, the escorting cruisers and destroyers fired star shells into the air and pointed their searchlights up as beacons to let the grateful pilots know where to go. The carriers again turned eastward as 116 planes coughed in to landings on their last precious drops of gasoline. Many gas tanks ran dry, however, before the planes could reach the carriers. A few, gliding in on empty tanks, crash-landed on the flight decks. As soon as the last plane landed, Mitscher turned his ships westward with searchlights ranging over the water, keeping a close lookout for survivors from the 80 downed planes. These had carried about 200 pilots and crewmen. More than 150 of these were rescued either during the night or early in the morning.

Spruance continued the pursuit on into June 21, but the delay to take on the returning planes, as well as the search for survivors, had so slowed the American fleet that the Japanese were now 360 miles away. Spruance therefore turned eastward, back to the Marianas. The Battle of the Philippine Sea was over.

Converging on the Philippines

A Debate on Strategy

BY MIDSUMMER of 1944, American land, naval, and air strength was firmly established in the Marianas and at the western tip of New Guinea. It now became necessary for the United States government to make a fundamental decision between two conflicting strategic plans.

General MacArthur, commanding in the Southwest Pacific, and

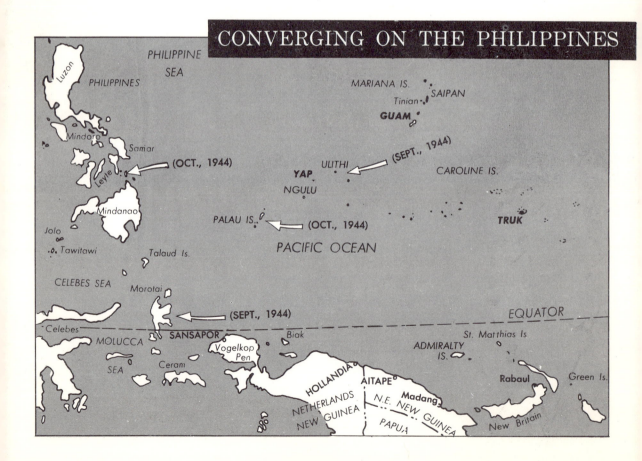

CONVERGING ON THE PHILIPPINES

Admiral Chester Nimitz.

General George C. Marshall, Chief of Staff of the United States Army, believed that the forces of the Central Pacific and Southwest Pacific should be combined to invade the Philippines and completely cut Japanese sea communications with the Southern Resources Area. They also felt that the Philippines would provide the best possible base for a final invasion of Japan.

Admiral Nimitz, however, with the support of Admiral Ernest J. King, Chief of Naval Operations, felt that it was unnecessary to invade the Philippines. The Navy thought it would be quicker and simpler to seize bases on the Japanese island of Formosa, or on the east coast of China, from which to make the final assault on Japan.

President Roosevelt and the Joint Chiefs of Staff met with Admiral Nimitz and General MacArthur in late July at Pearl Harbor to choose between these strategies. After Nimitz had presented his ideas to the President, MacArthur explained why he thought the advance should go by way of the Philippines. He pointed out that an assault on fortified Formosa would be much more dangerous and would suffer far more casualties than would an attack on the larger land mass of the Philippines, where the Americans would be helped by a friendly population. Finally, he reminded the President that America had an obligation to liberate the loyal Filipino people from ruthless Japanese occupation.

The military reasoning and the eloquence of General MacArthur persuaded both Admiral William D. Leahy, President Roosevelt's Chief of Staff, and the President himself. The Army strategy — an advance through the Philippines — was adopted.

Preliminary Operations

As soon as a decision was reached, Admiral Nimitz and the Navy supported the new strategy with as much enthusiasm and energy as if they had won the argument. In close cooperation, the Army and Navy staffs worked out the necessary plans.

These were to be carried out in three steps. First, Southwest Pacific forces would seize bases in the Halmahera Islands, while at the same time the Central Pacific elements assaulted the Palaus. The next step would be landings on the southern Philippine island of Mindanao and on the Japanese stronghold of Yap. Finally, in late December, 1944, a combined landing would be made on Leyte, in the central Philippines. Once Leyte was secured, MacArthur's assault forces would move northward into the main island of Luzon, probably around March of 1945.

In August, Admiral Nimitz placed Admiral Halsey in command of Central Pacific operational forces. The Third Fleet staff had completed its operations in the Solomons. At the same time, Nimitz wanted Admirals Spruance and Turner, and General Smith, and their staffs, to prepare plans for landings on Iwo Jima and Okinawa.

So the ships and men that had previously been known as the Fifth Fleet were now designated the Third Fleet; but except for a new commander and staff, there was practically no change in the organization. Admiral Mitscher's Fast Carrier Task Force simply became known as Task Force 38 instead of Task Force 58. Vice Admiral Theodore Wilkinson, commander of the Third Amphibious Force, took over practically all of the vessels and sailors that had been in Turner's Fifth Amphibious Force.

On September 15, 1944, Southwest Pacific troops landed on the island of Morotai in the Halmahera Islands. On the same day, the Third Amphibious Force landed the 1st Marine Division on the island of Peleliu in the Palaus. Opposition was light on Morotai, but the Marines had a tough job clearing the Japanese from Peleliu by October 13.

In support, Admiral Halsey and Task Force 38 had performed the usual carrier strikes to neutralize nearby bases and to soften up the enemy defenses. First they had hit Yap, Ulithi, and the Palaus on September 6, then swept the coast of the Philippines. Between September 9 and September 13, the American carrier planes had ranged almost unhindered, so Admiral Halsey had sent a message to Nimitz recommending that the proposed landings on Yap and Mindanao be abandoned, since they no longer seemed necessary. He had recommended, instead, that the landing on Leyte take place as soon as possible.

Nimitz sent Halsey's recommendation on to the Joint Chiefs of Staff, who were meeting with the British Chiefs of Staff at Quebec. Nimitz offered to send his XXIV Corps and Third Amphibious Force

43

to fight under MacArthur at Leyte. The Combined Chiefs of Staff at once requested General MacArthur's views.

MacArthur and his staff knew that an amphibious operation usually takes two months to prepare, but in the light of Halsey's recommendation, and Nimitz' offer of troops and ships, MacArthur informed the Joint Chiefs of Staff that he would be able to make the landing on Leyte on October 20 — only thirty-five days away.

The Sho *Plan*

AMERICAN submarine and air attacks against Japanese merchant shipping — and particularly against their scarce tankers — had caused an acute shortage of fuel oil and gasoline in Japan. Admiral Toyoda had therefore stationed most of the Combined Fleet on the coast of Borneo or in nearby Singapore, where fuel oil was plentiful. But because Japan was feverishly trying to train a new crop of carrier pilots, most of the Japanese aircraft carriers were in the Inland Sea of Japan. Here they could take on the new planes being rushed from the production lines of Japanese factories, and could continue with the training of the new carrier groups. All remaining Japanese tankers were being used to rush fuel oil and gasoline northward for these carriers and planes.

Because of the fuel shortage, flying hours for new pilot training were greatly reduced. As a result, by the fall of 1944, few of the pilots of Japanese army and navy planes were even as experienced as those who had been so disastrously defeated in the Battle of the Philippine Sea.

Meanwhile, Japanese Imperial Headquarters had prepared a plan for a last-ditch defense of the still far–flung Japanese Empire. This was called the "*Sho*" (Victory) Plan. The Japanese high command realized that if the Americans seized the Philippines, or Formosa, or the Ryukyus, or landed in the main islands of Japan, the empire would be split in two. The Southern Resources Area would be completely cut off from the home islands. The main body of the fleet could not receive ammunition, equipment, or replacements. Japan could receive no more fuel for ships, planes, or tanks. Defeat would be inevitable. For this reason, the *Sho* Plan would be an all-or-nothing gamble with the entire Combined Fleet, supported by all available air and ground strength.

The *Sho* Plan was to be carried out by having the separated fleet units converge from north and south to strike any American beachhead and to overwhelm the amphibious force supporting the landings. This would be done while one portion of the Japanese fleet acted as a decoy to lure the powerful American Fast Carrier Task Force away from the beachhead area.

The Battle off Formosa

EARLY IN OCTOBER, the American Third Fleet sailed northwestward from its new base anchorage at Ulithi to carry out a series of preliminary air strikes. At the same time, land-based planes — Fifth Air Force from New Guinea; Seventh from the Marianas — began to hammer at all Japanese bases within reach. Long-range B-29 "Superfortress" bombers from China attacked Formosa.

After bombing shipping and shore installations in and around Okinawa, Task Force 38 next turned its attention to Formosa. Despite the loss of many planes, the Japanese struck back fiercely. During the night of October 13-14, the American cruisers USS *Canberra* and USS *Houston* were badly damaged by torpedo plane attacks, and several others were hit. In addition to fires on these American

45

ships, the ocean was dotted with the flames of numerous Japanese planes that had been shot down. Returning Japanese pilots mistakenly thought these were sinking American ships.

Soon after this, Halsey's radio monitors intercepted jubilant Japanese reports of a great victory. Halsey thought that if they believed this, the Japanese high command might send the Combined Fleet out to pursue. He thought that if Japanese patrol planes saw the two damaged cruisers, limping slowly eastward, this might lure them into battle. So, leaving one carrier group to provide cover for the cruisers, he sailed out into the Philippine Sea with the rest of the Third Fleet.

Toyoda took the bait. He sent his newly trained carrier groups from their carriers in the Inland Sea to Formosa airfields to help complete the "destruction" of the American fleet. At the same time, Vice Admiral Kiyohide Shima's Second Strike Force of three cruisers and four destroyers was sent from the Ryukyu Islands to finish off the "remaining enemy elements."

Halsey then steamed back toward Formosa. On October 15 and 16, his carrier planes destroyed at least half of the six hundred Japanese carrier planes, wrecking the air groups beyond repair. Shima's Second Attack Force, however, withdrew from the trap in time and returned to the Ryukyus undamaged.

This ended the Battle off Formosa. American losses had been two cruisers badly damaged, several others less badly hit, and 76 aircraft shot down. American planes had destroyed more than 650 Japanese planes and damaged many others, as well as wrecking numerous shore installations.

The Return to the Philippines

ON OCTOBER 19, Admiral Barbey's and Admiral Wilkinson's Seventh

Seamen gunners watch intently as a graceful but powerful F4U "Corsair" leaves the carrier deck for a combat mission.

and Third Amphibious Forces converged in the waters of the Philippine Sea, a few hundred miles east of Leyte. Together they had more than 700 vessels transporting and protecting 200,000 American troops of Lieutenant General Walter Krueger's Sixth Army. Two days earlier, Rangers had landed on small islands off Leyte Gulf in order to protect the entry of the American fleet.

The combined amphibious forces were commanded by Vice Admiral Kinkaid, whose Seventh Fleet was given overall responsibility for support and protection of the operation. Kinkaid's fleet also had two principal combat elements. One was a surface force under Rear Admiral J. B. Oldendorf: six of the old battleships that had been damaged at Pearl Harbor, four heavy cruisers, four light cruisers, and twenty-six destroyers. The air support group, under Rear Admiral T. L. Sprague, consisted of sixteen escort carriers, nine destroyers, and eleven destroyer escorts.

Further out to sea was Admiral Halsey's Third Fleet, built around Mitscher's Fast Carrier Task Force — eight heavy carriers, eight light carriers, six fast battleships, three heavy cruisers, nine light cruisers, and fifty-eight destroyers. Mitscher had over one thousand carrier-based planes.

Kinkaid was responsible directly to General MacArthur for all direct naval support and protection of the land assault forces. Halsey, on the other hand, was still directly under the command of Admiral Nimitz, who had ordered him to give all possible assistance to Kinkaid. At the same time, Nimitz had told Halsey that his principal mission was to attack and destroy the main Japanese fleet, should it come out to do battle or otherwise try to interfere with the landings. There seemed to be no conflict between these two missions — first, to fight the Japanese fleet; second, to assist the landing operation — but this was because neither Nimitz nor Halsey had guessed the Japanese plan.

American sailors are buried at sea from a Coast Guard-manned assault transport.

THE BATTLE FOR LEYTE GULF

OCTOBER 23-26, 1944

Luzon Strait

Cape Engaño

JAPANESE THIRD FLEET ADM. OZAWA

BATTLE OFF CAPE ENGAÑO OCT 25

Luzon

Lingayen Gulf

THIRD FLEET

Bataan

MANILA

AIR ATTACKS

Corregidor

AIR ATTACKS OCT. 24

San Bernardino Strait

MC CAIN'S TASK GROUP

OCT. 25

Mindoro

Samar

BATTLE OFF SAMAR OCT. 25

1ST ATTACK FORCE

Sibuyan

(ADM. KURITA)

Panay

Cebu

Leyte

Leyte Gulf

Palawan

2ND ATTACK FORCE

(ADM. SHIMA)

AMERICAN BEACHHEAD

SEVENTH FLEET ADM. KINKAID

Negros

BATTLE OF SURIGAO STRAIT OCT. 25

SULU SEA

C FORCE

(ADM. NISHIMURA)

Mindanao

The Battle for Leyte Gulf

Initiation of Operation Sho

EARLY ON OCTOBER 17, Admiral Toyoda ordered the Combined Fleet to carry out the *Sho* Plan. Accordingly, four Japanese task forces converged on the Philippines. The First Attack Force, commanded by Vice Admiral Takeo Kurita and based near Singapore, moved north by way of Borneo toward the Sibuyan Sea and San Bernardino Strait. This force consisted of five battleships, ten heavy cruisers, two light cruisers, and fifteen destroyers — most of the Japanese surface naval strength. At the same time, east of Palawan Island was "C" Force, under Vice Admiral Shoji Nishimura, heading for Leyte Gulf via the Sulu Sea, the Mindanao Sea, and Surigao Strait. Nishimura had two battleships, one heavy cruiser, and four destroyers.

Meanwhile, Admiral Shima's Second Attack Force — originally intended as the decoy — moved from the Ryukyus for the South China Sea by way of the Formosa Strait and the Pescadores Islands. Shima had one light and two heavy cruisers, and four destroyers. The fourth task force was Admiral Ozawa's Mobile Force, moving southward from Japan's Inland Sea toward Luzon by way of the Philippine Sea. This once-proud carrier striking force was now reduced to one heavy carrier, three light carriers, two battleship-carriers (battleships to which flight decks had been added), three light cruisers, and ten destroyers.

As a result of the disastrous Battle off Formosa, Toyoda had been forced to make one change in his plans. Ozawa's Mobile Force had no more trained carrier air groups, and so was no longer the main striking force of the *Sho* Plan. Ozawa was carrying 160 airplanes with partially trained pilots. These were to fly off to attack the American beachhead, and then to land on airfields in the Philippines; they were not sufficiently trained to be able to return to the carriers. The Mobile Force was then to act as the decoy which would attract Halsey away from Leyte, thus permitting the three surface squadrons to strike a decisive blow against the beachhead and also against the convoys afloat in Leyte Gulf. Nishimura and Shima were to reach Leyte Gulf, via Surigao Strait, shortly before dawn. Kurita, with the Japanese main effort, was to converge from the north about an hour later.

During the morning of October 23, American submarines patrolling off Palawan, sighted the First Attack Force, reported it to Kinkaid, and then attacked. They sank two heavy cruisers and damaged a third so severely that it was forced to turn back with an escort of two destroyers.

During the remainder of the day, other American submarines and aircraft sighted both the First and Second Attack Forces, but inflicted no more damage upon either of these. Still unaware of the extent of the Japanese threat, on October 23 Admiral Halsey sent one of his four task groups of four carriers, commanded by Rear Admiral John S. McCain, back to Ulithi to rest, refuel, and rearm after the Battle off Formosa.

October 24

EARLY ON THE MORNING OF October 24, American search planes located Kurita's fleet entering the Sibuyan Sea, and Nishimura's C Force off the north coast of Mindanao. While American Third Fleet carrier planes struck repeatedly against the Japanese First Attack Force, aircraft from the Seventh Fleet's escort carriers attacked Nishimura's squadron in the eastern Sulu Sea. Admiral Kinkaid alerted Admiral Oldendorf's surface force of battleships, cruisers,

40,000 ton Japanese battleship Yamato.

and destroyers to prepare for a night action at the northern entrance of Surigao Strait.

The American carrier planes striking the two Japanese squadrons in the western waters of the Philippines were unopposed in the air. Although the warships maneuvered violently and protected themselves with curtains of antiaircraft fire, the skilled American pilots scored hit after hit.

Third Fleet planes concentrated their efforts against the two superbattleships *Musashi* and *Yamato*, but all of the Japanese ships were attacked time and again. Finally, at 3:30 P.M., Kurita ordered his fleet westward in the Sibuyan Sea. Halsey's pilots reported that the Japanese were retreating from San Bernardino Strait. They renewed their attacks against the stricken *Musashi*. At dusk, having

53

taken sixteen bomb hits and ten torpedoes, the great ship sank with about half her crew of two thousand men.

Nishimura's C Force, subjected to a slightly less intensive attack, had one battleship and a destroyer badly damaged, but the squadron continued into the Mindanao Sea. Shima's squadron had not been attacked.

Although they were not covering their approaching naval squadrons, the Japanese airmen had been busy. During the morning, planes based on Luzon struck repeatedly at the Third Fleet. The American carrier fighters knocked down most of the attackers, with small losses themselves. But one skillful Japanese pilot eluded the defensive screen and dropped a large bomb on the flight deck of the light carrier USS *Princeton,* damaging it severely. As other ships circled close to help put out fires and to rescue the carrier's crew, they were riddled by steel fragments from explosions in the carrier. The cruiser USS *Birmingham* was particularly hurt, and lost more than two hundred men killed and twice as many wounded.

In the late afternoon, American patrol planes sighted Admiral Ozawa's squadron approaching the east coast of Luzon from the northeast. When Halsey received reports that this enemy force contained four carriers and two battleships, he immediately assumed it to be the principal Japanese striking force. Halsey believed that his main mission was to destroy the most important part of the Japanese fleet, and so he immediately ordered all of Task Force 38 northward to engage Ozawa. Since Kurita seemed to be retreating westward in the Sibuyan Sea, Halsey did not think he needed to do anything about his secondary mission: helping Kinkaid protect the beachhead. He sent a message to McCain to refuel at sea, and to return promptly to join in the battle. The Japanese decoy was working.

Kinkaid, meanwhile, had understood from earlier messages that

Halsey was leaving a force of four battleships and four carriers to guard San Bernardino Strait, so he gave no further thought to the possible threat of Kurita's squadron. He devoted all of his attention to Japanese forces approaching from the southwest.

The Battle of Surigao Strait

SHORTLY BEFORE MIDNIGHT, Nishimura's C Force entered Surigao Strait. Shima's Second Attack Force was about thirty minutes behind him. Strangely, the two Japanese admirals had made no effort to coordinate their advance or their attack.

Nishimura's ships were soon attacked by a swarm of waiting American PT boats. The alert Japanese, however, avoided the torpedoes, sank one PT boat, and damaged three others. They continued northward in the darkness, evidently still expecting to surprise the Americans in Leyte Gulf. About halfway up the strait, however, American destroyer squadrons were steaming silently southward down each side of the strait, hidden from Japanese radar by the shoreline on either side. The destroyers torpedoed and sank Nishimura's flagship, the battleship *Yamashiro*, and one destroyer. The other three destroyers were damaged.

The battleship *Fuso*, the heavy cruiser *Mogami*, and the three damaged destroyers continued toward the mouth of the strait. It was almost 4:00 A.M. Then, at a range of fifteen thousand yards, Oldendorf's battleships and cruisers opened up on the five remaining Japanese ships. In a few moments the *Fuso* was sinking, the *Mogami* was knocked out of control, and two more Japanese destroyers were sunk. During the confused exchange of fire, one American destroyer was also hit and put out of action by shells from both American and Japanese ships.

Shima's Second Attack Force was now running the gauntlet of the American PT boats. His light cruiser was knocked out of action, but the two heavy cruisers and the destroyers continued north. Shortly after this, Shima passed the surviving destroyer of Nishimura's squadron, and though the two ships exchanged recognition signals, the destroyer did not report the destruction of the rest of C Force.

As he passed the center of the strait, Shima's radar detected some supposed targets to the north, and the Japanese ships turned to fire torpedoes at some rocky islands. In the haze and smoke of this maneuver, Shima's flagship rammed the damaged cruiser *Mogami*, and at this point Shima apparently began to realize that something was seriously wrong. With speed reduced as a result of the accident, he turned southward and steamed out of the strait. The Battle of Surigao Strait was over.

The Battle off Samar

SHORTLY AFTER DARK on the evening of October 24, Admiral Kurita had reversed course again, to head back toward San Bernardino Strait. He had expected to find American warships waiting for him there, but he was determined to fight his way through, to carry out his orders as best he could. Although the attacks he had received the previous day from the American planes, combined with the necessity for reversing his course for several hours, had seriously delayed him, he had hoped to join Nishimura in Leyte Gulf before noon on October 25.

To his amazement, Kurita found no American ambush at San Bernardino Strait when he passed through about 3:00 A.M. The Japanese sped south along the east coast of Samar. At dawn they sighted American planes, and then American ships. This was the northernmost element of the Seventh Fleet, consisting of six escort carriers, three destroyers, and four destroyer escorts, commanded by Rear Admiral C. A. F. Sprague, but the Japanese thought they had surprised part of Halsey's Third Fleet. They opened fire at extreme range and closed in, expecting to destroy part of the Fast Carrier Task Force, even though they felt certain they would suffer severely themselves.

The American carrier group, even more surprised than the Japanese, immediately turned to flee. But they were much slower than the Japanese warships and, in addition, as they headed eastward into the wind at top speed, launching their planes for an attack, they were outlined for a while against the rising sun. Then intermittent rain squalls blurred the targets for the Japanese.

While the Japanese battleships followed directly behind the fleeing escort carriers, the Japanese cruisers and destroyers began to swing around the flanks of the carrier group, but the damage they had suffered in the previous day's attacks had seriously injured the fire-control systems of many of the Japanese ships. Poor Japanese gunnery, together with the rain and excellent American seamanship, worked to the advantage of the carrier group. It escaped serious damage for nearly an hour.

By this time the little carriers had launched all of their planes, and these were striking vigorously at the pursuing ships. As the Japanese closed in, Admiral Sprague ordered his destroyers and destroyer escorts to attack with torpedoes. Gallantly the seven small ships turned to face a hail of fire from four battleships, eight cruisers, and eleven destroyers. Three of the small American ships were sunk, two were severely damaged, and two escaped with light damage. But their torpedoes put one Japanese cruiser out of action, and the bold attack delayed the Japanese pursuit, for the big ships had to maneuver constantly to escape torpedoes.

When the American destroyer attack was over, however, the Japanese pressed on again toward the American carriers, which now began to take numerous hits. One had been sunk, and the others were suffering severe punishment when the Japanese were attacked by all of the planes from another escort carrier group. Although there were less than sixty planes in this attack, they succeeded in crippling two more heavy cruisers, and forced the Japanese battleships to scatter temporarily to escape their torpedoes.

By this time the Japanese ships had become badly spread out and were in some confusion. Kurita knew that many American planes had been shot down, but he still thought that he was engaging at least part of Halsey's Third Fleet, and expected a massive air strike at any moment. Earlier in the morning he had received a message which indicated to him that C Force had been badly hurt, and now he was receiving messages from Ozawa that he was engaged with the Third Fleet. In addition, Japanese radio operators were intercepting messages from Kinkaid asking Halsey for help. Confused and exhausted, Kurita decided to turn north to help Ozawa against Halsey's main body. He thought that Task Force 38 was only a few miles away, and that his surface ships should be able to reach the American carriers while their planes were off on strike against Ozawa.

Kurita has been accused of cowardice, or of gross inefficiency, for turning away to the northward just as his far superior fleet was less than two hours from Leyte Gulf. He could probably have sunk every American escort carrier, even though he would have taken additional losses himself. His striking power would probably still have been considerably superior to that of the six old battleships of Kinkaid's Seventh Fleet, for these had used up practically all of their ammunition in supporting the troops on shore, and in their action against Nishimura's squadron at Surigao Strait. It is possible that Kurita could have destroyed literally hundreds of defenseless American

58

merchant ships, and might well have caused so much damage as to completely ruin MacArthur's invasion.

Though Kurita's critics are probably correct in estimating how much damage he could have caused, his error was an honest one. He felt that by joining with Ozawa he could do the most harm to the United States fleet. But the morning passed, and he did not make contact with Halsey's ships. Moreover, he had begun to suffer ever-increasing punishment, first from long-range strikes of Admiral McCain's task group, and then from the carrier group returning with Halsey from the north. It was then that Kurita realized his error, but by this time it was too late to remedy it. All he could do was to turn west, and retreat through San Bernardino Strait.

The Battle off Samar did not end with the disappearance of Kurita's fleet. Despite the severe losses that they had taken in their attacks against the American fleets the previous day, Japanese land-based planes had returned fiercely to combat early on October 25. They added considerably to the punishment that the Seventh Fleet ships took that day. Most serious of all, some of the Japanese pilots, their planes loaded with bombs, dove directly into American ships. They killed themselves, of course, but they also killed and wounded many American sailors and inflicted severe damage on the American ships. They sank one escort carrier in this way, and damaged numerous others.

This was the beginning of the Japanese *Kamikaze* ("Divine Wind") tactics. Untrained Japanese pilots, unable to fight the skilled Americans in the air, volunteered to crash their planes into American ships, willingly committing suicide to strike a blow for the defense of their country. These first suicide pilots did not affect the outcome of the battle, but Americans would see much more of the *Kamikazes* in the months to come.

59

The Battle off Cape Engaño

SHORTLY AFTER DAWN on October 25, while Halsey's Third Fleet was continuing its northward rush, Admiral Mitscher sent out planes to find Ozawa's squadron. A little after 8:00 A.M. these planes sighted the Japanese vessels. They immediately shot down the twenty planes that Ozawa had kept with his squadron for fighter defense. They then closed in upon the surface vessels. This was the beginning of a day of horror for Ozawa's Mobile Force. By evening all four carriers were sunk, along with some of the other ships. All the remaining ships were damaged.

By midmorning, however, Halsey was beginning to receive a series of radio messages from Admiral Kinkaid, informing him that things were not going well near Leyte Gulf. Not realizing that the Seventh Fleet battleships were not in shape for combat, Halsey felt that Kinkaid was unnecessarily alarmed, but he ordered Admiral McCain, who had been refueled by the fast "sea train," to hurry as rapidly as possible to assist the Seventh Fleet. With Task Force 38, Halsey chased after the remnants of Ozawa's squadron.

At about 11:00 A.M., however, increasingly urgent messages from Kinkaid were followed by a radio message direct from Admiral Nimitz at Pearl Harbor, asking Halsey why his battleships were not helping the Seventh Fleet. Halsey, certain that he had acted properly, was furious to receive these messages suggesting that he had failed to give Kinkaid enough help at Leyte Gulf. But, although he was now only forty miles from the damaged Japanese vessels, he decided, after Nimitz' message, that he had better turn back with his battleships and one carrier group to help Kinkaid. He ordered Mitscher's two remaining carrier groups to finish off Ozawa's squadron. During the night and next day the carrier planes, and American submarines waiting east of the Ryukyus, picked off several more fleeing Japanese vessels. Only ten of Ozawa's nineteen ships limped back to Japanese home waters.

The Final Actions

MEANWHILE, near San Bernardino Strait, during the afternoon of October 25, Halsey's returning carriers had begun to hit Kurita's ships. Third Fleet planes — with some assistance from Seventh Fleet and Fifth Air Force aircraft — continued strike after strike for two more days before Kurita returned to the safety of his Borneo bases. To Halsey's intense disappointment, he had missed surface battles with both Ozawa and Kurita.

The Japanese navy had all but disappeared as an organized, fighting force. Its losses in the Battle for Leyte Gulf were one heavy carrier, three light carriers, three battleships, six heavy cruisers, four light cruisers, eleven destroyers, and one submarine. Almost every other ship had been damaged. More than 10,000 Japanese sailors were killed, plus at least 500 airmen who were shot down. American losses were one light carrier, two escort carriers, two destroyers, one destroyer escort, and more than two hundred aircraft, plus 2,800 Americans killed, and about 1,000 more wounded.

The Fleet and the *Kamikazes*

The Struggle for Air Control Over Leyte

THE NEW JAPANESE *Kamikaze* tactics around Leyte threatened American control of the air over an operational battle zone for the first time in two years. The Seventh Fleet's escort carriers had been temporarily knocked out of effective action by the punishment they had suffered in the Battle for Leyte Gulf. But in early November, the Fifth Air Force, from airfields on Leyte, gradually gained air superiority, with assistance from Third Fleet carrier planes.

By December, additional airfields had been built in the beachhead, and Admiral Kinkaid's escort carrier air groups had been strengthened sufficiently to return to action. The Third Fleet was able to withdraw to Ulithi for two weeks of rest, repair, reinforcement, and resupply. Shortly after this the Seventh Fleet supported a successful amphibious landing on the west coast of Leyte, despite severe damage inflicted by *Kamikazes*.

On to Luzon

A WEEK LATER, the Third and Seventh fleets supported the next step on General MacArthur's advance through the Philippines: a landing on Mindoro. The purpose of this daring thrust deep into the heart of the Japanese-held Philippines was to establish air bases to support the next move against Luzon itself.

Early in January, the Fast Carrier Task Force began hammering at Japanese air bases on Luzon, Formosa, and the Ryukyus. At the same time, the entire Seventh Fleet — seven hundred warships and transports of all kinds — was steaming through the central Philippines

LST is hit by Japanese bombers in the Philippines.

toward the western coast of Luzon. As the leading warships entered
the Sulu Sea, the *Kamikazes* began a series of vicious attacks. One
escort carrier was sunk, and several battleships, cruisers, and destroyers were severely damaged. American land-based planes stepped up

their attacks against Japanese air bases, and the Fast Carrier Task Force, then off the coast of Formosa, hastened back to enter the battle for air superiority over Luzon.

By January 8, all the Japanese air bases had been neutralized, though an occasional *Kamikaze* still tried to strike at the advancing fleet. When American troops stormed ashore in Lingayen Gulf on January 9, there was no air opposition.

Moving cautiously into Lingayen Gulf, the Seventh Fleet had received help from another source. During the preceding week, Filipino guerrillas in rowboats had painstakingly cleared away more than four hundred Japanese mines in a crude minesweeping operation.

The Cruise of the Third Fleet

WITH GENERAL MACARTHUR'S troops ashore on western Luzon, and the air and naval situations now controlled by the Seventh Fleet and the Fifth Air Force, Halsey and his Third Fleet turned to other targets. After completing the interrupted raid against Formosa, he led the Fast Carrier Task Force into the South China Sea. The carrier planes struck the Japanese-held coasts of China and Indochina, destroying land installations, roads, railroads, Japanese merchant ships and warships, and several hundred planes.

Japanese planes were waiting to strike the American fleet as it returned through the narrow Luzon Strait on January 21. Combined conventional and *Kamikaze* attacks damaged three carriers and several smaller ships, but the Americans easily beat off the attacks with heavy losses, and pounded Formosa again. Halsey then returned to Ulithi, to turn the Central Pacific operational forces back over to Admiral Spruance. The Third Fleet again became the Fifth Fleet, and Mitscher's task force resumed its old title of Task Force 58.

LSM's (Landing Ship, Medium) dash for the beach at Iwo Jima, loaded with Marines of the Fifth Amphibious Corps.

Iwo Jima

WHILE the Third Fleet had been fighting in the waters off the Philippines, Admiral Spruance and his staff had been preparing for the two final amphibious operations of the Central Pacific Theater. The first of these was to be the seizure of Iwo Jima, in the Volcano Islands. In January, in order to exercise closer control over this operation and the later invasion of Okinawa, Admiral Nimitz moved his headquarters from Pearl Harbor to Guam.

Iwo Jima was located on the direct air route between the Marianas bases of the Twentieth Air Force B-29's and their principal targets in Japan. The Japanese bombers from the tiny island had raided the Superfortress fields on Guam, Saipan, and Tinian. Japanese fighter planes on Iwo were also attacking the B-29's both going and coming as the American planes continued their strikes against Japan. Japanese attacks were reduced, but not stopped, by heavy bombing attacks on the island by the Seventh and Twentieth Air Forces from the Marianas.

D-Day, Iwo Jima. U.S. Marines swarm over the beaches.

In February, as a preliminary to an assault on Iwo Jima, Spruance and Mitscher led Task Force 58 on a raid to the very heart of the Japanese Empire. On February 16 and 17, despite bad weather, American carrier planes struck airfields around Tokyo, while at Iwo itself the battleships and cruisers of the amphibious support force were laying down the heaviest naval gunfire bombardment probably ever concentrated on an area of eight square miles. On February 18, the carrier planes of returning Task Force 58 added to the bombardment.

During the night of February 18-19, the expeditionary force arrived off the tiny island. It included 495 ships, and more than 350 carrier planes on the supporting escort carriers. The assault force itself consisted of 75,000 Marines of the V Amphibious Corps, with 36,000 additional Army troops to take over the island once it was secured.

On the morning of February 19, the assault began. Despite the intensity of the preliminary bombardment, the Japanese had been well sheltered in their underground caves and massive concrete blockhouses. The battle raged for four weeks. By the time it was over, 23,000 defenders had been killed, while the Marines had lost 4,500 killed, and more than 16,000 wounded. In addition, the naval support forces, which had sustained repeated *Kamikaze* attacks from Japanese bases, lost 1 escort carrier sunk, 30 other ships damaged, and 168 aircraft shot down. Naval losses were 176 killed, and almost 1,100 wounded.

But the capture of Iwo Jima proved to be worth the severe losses suffered by the attackers. Before the end of the war, more than 2,000 B-29's made emergency landings on the island; most of these planes would otherwise have been lost. Thus more than 20,000 American lives were saved by the capture of this island.

Rockets streak from an LCI toward the beaches of Okinawa prior to the American invasion of the island.

Okinawa

THE NEXT OBJECTIVE for Admiral Spruance's Fifth Fleet was the Ryukyu island of Okinawa. As soon as Iwo Jima was secured, the Fast Carrier Task Force moved north again to attack the Japanese main islands, particularly Kyushu, in preparation for the invasion scheduled early in April. Then, on March 23, the carriers added their powerful striking force to the long-range Army bombers already softening up Okinawa.

During the last week of March, convoys of the joint expeditionary force coming from Hawaii, from the Philippines, from the South

Pacific, and even from the west coast of the United States, began to converge in the Western Pacific. They carried approximately 200,000 troops of the Tenth Army, commanded by Lieutenant General Simon B. Buckner, Jr. Another 200,000 men accompanied the force: garrison troops, supply units, engineers for airfield construction, and base personnel for the many airfields that the Americans planned to build on the island. Amongst the 1,213 ships of Admiral Turner's Joint Expeditionary Force were 318 warships, including 10 battleships, 9 heavy cruisers, 4 light cruisers, 23 destroyers, and 14 escort carriers carrying 564 planes. These were in addition to the 83 ships and 920 aircraft of the Fast Carrier Task Force, and a newly arrived British carrier force of 22 ships and 244 planes.

On March 26, as a preliminary to the main landings, the 77th Infantry Division was landed on the Kerama Islands west of Okinawa to provide an advance naval anchorage and seaplane base. The in-

One of the battleships raised from the mud at Pearl Harbor lashes Japanese installations on Okinawa in support of Army and Marine landings on the island.

vasion forces received an unexpected dividend from this landing, since the Japanese had secretly based 350 suicide motorboats in the Keramas, and all of these were captured or destroyed. Had these been able to operate against the convoys of the expeditionary force, many ships would have been sunk, and thousands of American lives lost.

On April 1, following a tremendous air and naval bombardment, the III Marine Amphibious Corps and the Army's XXIV Corps stormed ashore along an eight-mile stretch near Hagushi, on the southwest coast of the island. Although the Japanese offered no resistance to the initial landing, the Americans soon ran into fanatically defended, powerful fortifications covering the southern portion of the island.

A United States battleship fires salvos into the beach of Okinawa just before Army and Marine landings.

The Last Blow of the Japanese Navy

ON APRIL 6, in accordance with a previously prepared Japanese defensive plan, the attacking American ground troops and the supporting naval vessels were struck by an intensive air attack that lasted for nearly thirty-six hours. More than 1,000 Japanese planes took part, of which about 350 were *Kamikazes*. The suicide planes concentrated against the American warships, while the other Japanese aircraft engaged the defensive fighter screen of the American carriers. By the time this terrific air battle was over, nearly 400 Japanese planes had been shot down, but 30 American ships had been sunk or badly damaged.

Under cover of this violent air conflict, the remnants of the Japanese fleet sailed out of the Inland Sea for one more battle. One of these vessels was the giant battleship *Yamato*, accompanied by one cruiser and eight destroyers. Admiral Toyoda realized that this would be a suicide mission. There could be no later naval battles, he knew, since these ships carried the last fuel oil to be found in Japan. Commanding the squadron was Vice Admiral Seiichi Ito.

Watchful American submarines sighted the vessels off the east coast of Kyushu, late on April 6, and flashed a warning to Admiral Spruance. The next morning planes from Task Force 58 struck from the sky in overwhelming force. Without air cover, the only protection for the Japanese ships was their own evasive maneuvers and antiaircraft fire. But for the skilled, veteran American pilots the task was simple. The *Yamato*, taking the brunt of the American attack, was hit repeatedly. It soon sank as did also the cruiser and four destroyers. The remaining four destroyers, all damaged, fled back to the protection of the Inland Sea. The Japanese navy had ceased to exist.

71

The Fleet Can "Take It"

THE WAR AT SEA was not yet over, however. For the next two months, on an average of once a week, the Japanese launched mass air attacks, with the *Kamikazes* playing a central role. In these ten great air battles, more than 4,000 Japanese planes were destroyed. About half of these were *Kamikazes*. Thirty-six American ships were sunk, and 368 damaged. The largest vessel sunk was a destroyer, but 10 battleships, 13 carriers, 5 cruisers, and 67 more destroyers required extensive repairs. About 5,000 American sailors were killed, and an equal number wounded in these attacks.

Spruance and his fleet stayed on the job and fought it out. He knew that his ships could deal with the *Kamikazes,* or any other Japanese air raiders, and defeat them, even though the fleet might suffer losses. In this way the Navy saved the lives of many of the hard-fighting ground soldiers and permitted them to win an early victory.

On land, by June 20, General Buckner's Tenth Army had conquered the island of Okinawa, even though Buckner himself had been killed two days before the last Japanese surrendered. By staying steadfastly at its thankless job at sea, the fleet had made a tremendous contribution to the victory on land.

WIDE WORLD PHOTO

A Japanese Kamikaze plane, hit by Navy gunners of Task Force 58, explodes in midair off Okinawa.

A Japanese Kamikaze pilot desperately aims his "Zero" fighter into the deck of the US battleship Missouri. Many Kamikaze volunteers were wired to the rudder pedals and had the hatches of their aircraft cockpits locked from the outside to prevent their escape at the last moment.

The War Under the Sea

The Opposing Submarine Fleets

AT THE OUTSET of the war, the Japanese and American submarine fleets in the Pacific were about evenly matched, but the Japanese had one tremendous advantage. Their "Long Lance" torpedoes were fast, accurate, and deadly. American torpedoes were much slower, were not reliable, and often, even when they struck their targets, would not explode.

The Americans had one advantage, but it only partly offset the Japanese torpedo superiority. The Americans had radar sets on their submarines, which helped them find targets and avoid air and surface attacks. During the war, as American scientists made startling strides in improving and refining radar, the latest and best equipment was mounted on American submarines. Later in the war, the Japanese began to use radar, but they were consistently behind the United States in this important field of electronic development.

Submarines had two main missions in the Pacific war. First, they were the eyes and the ears of the surface fleets, needed to detect and report enemy naval movements, and to attack enemy surface ships when they had a chance. Both Japanese and American submarines performed this mission well.

The second important use of submarines was against enemy supply lines. Germany in World War I, and again at the beginning of World War II, had shown that vigorous attacks against the merchant shipping of an enemy nation could seriously cripple its war effort. In addition, in a war fought across the vast reaches of an ocean, submarines could attack vessels carrying supplies and reinforcements to outlying island outposts, and would be particularly dangerous

74

against troop convoys undertaking amphibious invasions.

The Japanese, however, knew that United States industry was not vulnerable to attacks on its overseas supply lines, as Britain was. Accordingly, they decided that the best use they could make of their submarines would be in support of their fleet operations and attacks against American warships. They were not worried about their own supply lines between Japan and the Southern Resources Area because they did not believe that American submarines could penetrate far beyond their defensive perimeter in the Central and Southwest Pacific.

Early Operations with the Fleet

THE JAPANESE began submarine operations before dawn on December 7, in combination with their attack on Pearl Harbor. They used both midget and conventional submarines. The midget submarines, with their two-man crews, were attached to the larger submarines and carried to the vicinity of Pearl Harbor. There they were cut loose to try to get into the American anchorage. One got past the torpedo net, but was sunk by an alert American destroyer more than an hour before the Japanese air raid began. The Japanese lost four other midget submarines and one larger one during unsuccessful underseas attacks that day.

During the following year, the Japanese made a few other attempts to use their midget submarines, but most of these were unsatisfactory. Before the end of the year the Japanese had given up the midget submarine effort.

During 1942, also, a few Japanese submarines operated along the American Pacific coast. In June they created considerable excitement in the United States and in Canada by shelling Los Angeles, Astoria, and Vancouver Island. They caused very little damage, however, and apparently were not particularly interested in attacking American coastal shipping.

Both sides used submarines in the Battle of Midway. Admiral Yamamoto ordered a Japanese submarine screen established between Midway and Oahu. But the submarines did not get to their positions until June 1, after the American carrier task force had passed to take up its position north of Midway. The Japanese scouting mission failed completely, and Yamamoto was lulled into a false sense of security, believing that there were no American carriers in the Central Pacific. This submarine scouting failure contributed to the defeat of Yamamoto's Combined Fleet.

During the battle itself, the USS *Nautilus* popped up in the middle of Admiral Nagumo's Mobile Force, and was attacked by Japanese planes and warships. She eluded all attacks, however, and late in the afternoon was able to fire three torpedoes at the damaged Japanese carrier, *Kaga*. Although two of the torpedoes missed their target, one struck the burning carrier squarely on the side. But instead of exploding, the American torpedo broke in two; the warhead sank to the bottom of the sea, while the remainder of the torpedo floated beside the stricken vessel and was used as a life raft by survivors.

The most important submarine exploit of the Battle of Midway took place on June 6. The badly damaged American carrier USS *Yorktown* was being towed back to Pearl Harbor by American destroyers when she was sighted by the Japanese submarine *I-168*. The Japanese boat attacked immediately; one torpedo sank the destroyer *Hammann,* and another smashed into the wounded carrier, which soon sank. Thus the little *I-168* sank both of the American vessels lost during the Battle of Midway.

This Japanese submarine success was partially offset two months later, after the disastrous Allied defeat in the Battle of Savo Island, on August 9, 1942. On the day following the battle, the little American submarine *S-44* sank the Japanese heavy cruiser *Kako* on its way back to Rabaul from Savo Island.

Later, during the naval struggle for the control of the seas around the southeastern Solomons, Japanese submarines succeeded in sinking the carrier USS *Wasp*, the injured cruiser USS *Juneau*, the destroyers *O'Brien* and *Porter*, and severely damaging the battleship USS *North Carolina*.

Starting the Blockade of Japan

As DEFECTS in American torpedoes were slowly eliminated, and American submarine captains became more experienced, the rate of sinking of Japanese merchant ships began to rise. By the end of 1942, American submarines had sunk 670,000 tons of Japanese shipping.

During 1943, the rate of sinking of Japanese merchant ships — particularly tankers — rose sharply. Thus the Japanese began to feel the pinch on fuel oil for warships and gasoline for airplanes. By the middle of 1943, the Americans had finally overcome most of their torpedo troubles, and in the following months their toll of merchant shipping rose still more.

Belatedly, the Japanese initiated a system of convoys to restore better communications between the home islands and the Southern Resources Area. This convoy system, however, never became as efficient as that which the British and Americans had developed in the Atlantic.

To cope with the Japanese convoy escorts, the Americans adopted the German wolf-pack technique. But since the Japanese convoys were smaller and not as well organized as those the U-boats faced in the Atlantic, the Americans rarely had more than three submarines to any one wolf pack.

"Take Her Down!"

IN FEBRUARY, 1943, there occurred one of the most stirring incidents in America's naval history. The submarine *Growler,* patrolling near the Bismarcks, engaged in a surface night battle with a Japanese gunboat. Unexpectedly the Japanese vessel changed course, and the *Growler* rammed her. As the shaken submarine was attempting to back away, machine-gun fire from the gunboat sprayed her bridge, killing or wounding most of those on deck. The skipper, Commander Howard W. Gilmore, was seriously wounded, and unable to move. Gilmore ordered the four other survivors down the hatch into the submarine. Then, firmly, the stricken officer gave his last command: "Take her down!"

Gilmore was never seen again, but his heroism was rewarded after his death by the Congressional Medal of Honor.

Supporting the Pacific Offensives

THE MAIN THRUST of Admiral Nimitz' forces in the Central Pacific began in November of 1943, with the assault on the Gilbert islands of Tarawa and Makin. During the fight for Makin, the escort carrier *Liscome Bay* was sunk by a Japanese submarine, and 650 of her crew of 900 men were killed. Meanwhile, near Tarawa, another Japanese submarine was rammed and sunk by the destroyer USS *Frazer.*

While amphibious forces were assaulting the Gilberts, American submarines were scouting around Truk to report any Japanese effort to interfere with the American landings. The *Corvina* was sunk by a Japanese submarine. At about the same time, further east, the submarine *Sculpin* was attacked by the escort vessels of a Japanese convoy. A depth charge attack brought the injured submarine to the surface, where her crew continued the battle with their deck guns. Seeing the fight was hopeless, Captain John B. Cromwell ordered the vessel to be scuttled. Since he possessed important information about coming American invasion plans in the South Pacific, Cromwell feared that if he were captured the Japanese might torture this information from him. He therefore decided that he would go down with his vessel. He too, was awarded the Congressional Medal of Honor after his death.

Some time after this, the submarine *Sailfish* was patrolling off the coast of Japan when, shortly after midnight on December 4, 1943, she discovered a large target on her radar. Closing in, Lieutenant Commander R. E. Ward, her skipper, fired several torpedoes. Because of stormy weather, Ward was unable to get another shot until early morning. It was then that he first realized that his target was the Japanese carrier, *Chuyo*, and that he had damaged her with a torpedo. Stealthily closing in again, he fired a spread of torpedoes at the carrier. They hit and sank her immediately. Although vigorously attacked by the carrier's escorts, the submarine escaped.

As the American amphibious advance pushed into the Western Pacific, leaving Japanese outposts scattered behind in the Central and Southwest Pacific, the Japanese began to use their submarines to supply bypassed garrisons. There was nothing wrong with this, of course. The Americans had used submarines to supply Corregidor and Guadalcanal earlier in the war, and used them to send supplies to the Filipino guerrillas after that. The serious Japanese error was in failing at the same time to attack lengthening American supply lines.

Early in 1944, American submarines in the Pacific began to receive a new type of electric torpedo. These torpedoes were slightly slower, but much more reliable than the older torpedoes. Furthermore, they were much more quickly produced, thus making it easier to keep the growing American submarine fleet supplied with ammunition. Thanks to these new weapons, sinkings of Japanese merchant ships rose again during 1944, with the submarines accounting for more than half of the three million tons sunk that year.

The Final Battles

ONE OF THE MOST memorable exploits of the submarine war in the Pacific was performed in late May, 1944, by the destroyer escort USS *England*, in operations around the Bismarck and Admiralty islands. After the *England* had sunk six Japanese submarines in ten days, Admiral King sent a message from Washington: "There will always be an *England* in the United States Navy."

One reason for this great accumulation of Japanese submarines in the waters north of the Bismarcks and the Admiralties, was because Japan expected an American invasion of the Palau Islands. So the Japanese put a submarine screen in front of the Palaus.

As the Fifth Fleet headed toward the Marianas — instead of the Palaus — American submarines were active around the main Japanese fleet anchorage of Tawitawi and on the routes that the Japanese fleet would take to the Marianas. At the same time, an American wolf pack had discovered three small convoys of reinforcements and supplies heading toward Saipan. Between May 31 and June 5 these submarines sank seven ships, drowning about ten thousand Japanese soldiers and sending valuable supplies to the bottom.

During the days just prior to the Marianas invasion, the submarine *Harder*, operating off Tawitawi, sank three Japanese destroyers and damaged two more between June 6 and 9. Then on June 13, the *Redfin* reported on the departure of Admiral Ozawa's main fleet toward the Philippine Sea, giving Spruance the first warning that led to his preparations for the Battle of the Philippine Sea.

During the first day of that battle, two American submarines contributed greatly toward the American victory. The *Albacore* sank the aircraft carrier *Taiho*, Admiral Ozawa's flagship, while soon afterward the *Cavalla* sank the carrier *Shokaku*, the only remaining survivor of the attack on Pearl Harbor.

Four months later, on October 23, the American submarines *Darter* and *Dace* first reported the Japanese approach to Leyte Gulf. They then attacked Admiral Kurita's First Attack Force, sinking two heavy cruisers and damaging another. During the battle that followed, the submarine *Breen* damaged another Japanese heavy cruiser. Immediately afterward the *Jallao* sank the light cruiser *Tama*, and the *Halibut* sank a Japanese destroyer, both crippled survivors of the Battle off Cape Engaño.

On November 21, 1944, the USS *Sea Lion II* sank the *Kongo* — sole battleship to fall victim to American submarines. Then, on November 29, the USS *Archer Fish* discovered the supercarrier *Shinano*, sister ship to the giant battleships *Musashi* and *Yamato*, but lately converted into a carrier. The *Shinano*, heading south along the Honshu coast toward the Inland Sea, was hit by four torpedoes, and sank quickly because her inexperienced crew had failed to close her watertight bulkhead doors. These were the last major warships to be sunk by American submarines.

The last important submarine success of the war was achieved by the Japanese. On July 30, 1945, the American heavy cruiser *Indiana-*

polis was sunk in the Philippine Sea by an unidentified submarine.

American submarines in the Pacific sank more than 1,100 merchant ships, totaling 4,800,000 tons of shipping — over 56 per cent of the total of Japanese merchant shipping lost during the war. They also sank 201 warships, totaling 540,000 tons. Of these, the most important were 25 submarines (including 2 German U-boats), 39 destroyers, 9 light cruisers, 4 heavy cruisers, 1 battleship, and 8 aircraft carriers. In performing this tremendous effort, 52 American submarines were lost, most of them without a trace; unknown and unsung heroes of World War II.

JAPAN'S MERCHANT MARINE

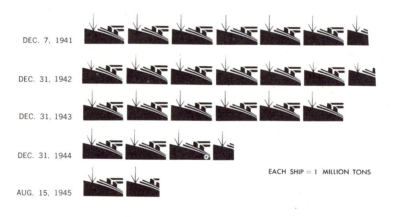

DEC. 7, 1941

DEC. 31, 1942

DEC. 31, 1943

DEC. 31, 1944

AUG. 15, 1945

EACH SHIP = 1 MILLION TONS

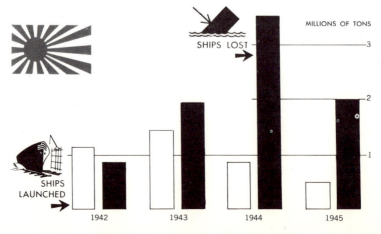

MILLIONS OF TONS

SHIPS LOST

3

2

1

SHIPS LAUNCHED

1942   1943   1944   1945

The Strangulation of Japan

Preparations for Invasion

DURING THE SUMMER of 1945, the staffs of General MacArthur and Admiral Nimitz completed plans for two massive invasions of the Japanese main islands. One of these was to take place in the fall of 1945, on the shores of the southern island of Kyushu. The other, scheduled for March of 1946, was to be on the Tokyo plain of Honshu.

While ground troops were preparing for these operations in the Philippines and on Okinawa, and while the Seventh Fleet was supporting numerous small Australian amphibious landings in the Netherlands East Indies, the blockade of Japan was being constantly tightened; the Japanese people were being more and more heavily punished.

Three main forces were accomplishing this preparation for the final onslaught against the Japanese Empire. The submarines continued their relentless and efficient scouring of the waters around Japan. The B-29's of the Twentieth Air Force struck repeatedly against Japanese industries, population centers, and lines of communication. And the Fast Carrier Task Force, after a brief rest from its long ordeal off Okinawa, came back to harry the coast and inland areas of Japan.

The Last Carrier Strikes

THESE CARRIER STRIKES began on July 10 with an intensive raid against Tokyo, and ended a month and five days later with another raid against that devastated city. Meanwhile, coordinating their strikes with the B-29 raids, the carrier planes ranged up and down

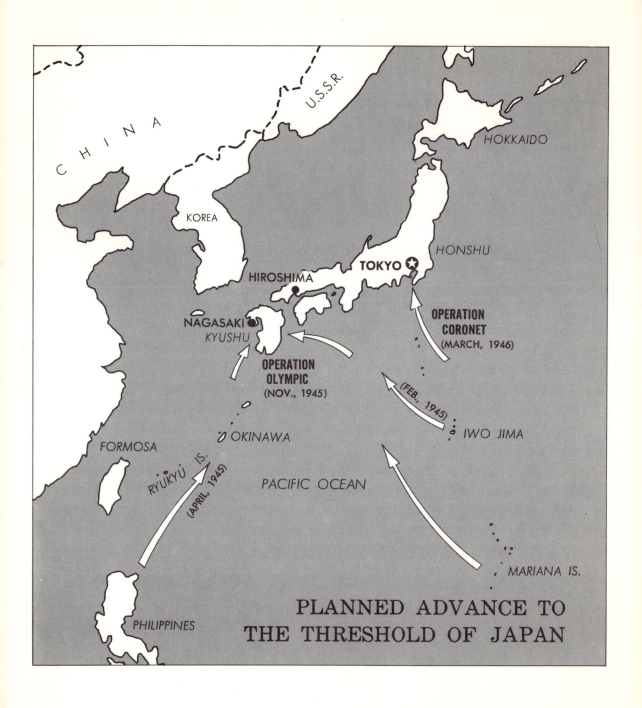

C H I N A

U.S.S.R.

HOKKAIDO

KOREA

HONSHU

HIROSHIMA

TOKYO ☆

NAGASAKI
KYUSHU

**OPERATION
CORONET**
(MARCH, 1946)

**OPERATION
OLYMPIC**
(NOV., 1945)

(FEB., 1945)

IWO JIMA

OKINAWA

FORMOSA

RYUKYU IS.

(APRIL, 1945)

PACIFIC OCEAN

MARIANA IS.

PHILIPPINES

PLANNED ADVANCE TO
THE THRESHOLD OF JAPAN

off the coast of Japan. At the same time, the battleships and cruisers of the Fast Carrier Task Force came closer to shore to carry out surface bombardments. In addition to the 94 vessels and more than 1,000 aircraft of Admiral Mitscher's Fast Carrier Task Force, a British carrier force of 28 vessels and 248 planes took part.

The Allies lost 362 planes, but sank one Japanese aircraft carrier, one battleship, two battleship-carriers, two heavy cruisers, four light cruisers, nine destroyers, and destroyed more than thirty-three hundred aircraft in the air or on the ground. These final strikes left Japan with a total of only fourteen major warships, all badly damaged: one heavy carrier, one light carrier, one escort carrier, one battleship, and ten destroyers.

Culmination of the Blockade

THESE RAIDS, also, resulted in the destruction of thousands of tons of shipping. The few Japanese merchant ships remaining afloat were mostly damaged. Those that could still operate had no fuel.

By early August of 1945, it was obvious to the Japanese government that it could not continue the war much longer. True enough there were still two million Japanese soldiers under arms in Japan, and almost as many more in Manchuria and China. There were also about seven thousand Japanese airplanes available to be used against the Allied forces closing in upon the Japanese Empire. But there were no pilots for these airplanes, and though suicide missions would be able to cause much damage to the Allies, it was now obvious that the *Kamikazes* could not repel an invasion. Furthermore, there would not be fuel enough for all of these planes to take the air.

The wheels of Japanese industry were grinding to a halt because no more raw materials were arriving by sea. Food was becoming scarce. Increasing numbers of people were made homeless by the

A black cat mascot strolls across the flight deck of a British aircraft carrier. As shown by its wake, the ship is weaving to avoid prowling enemy submarines.

continued Allied bombing raids. Then came the atomic bombs on Hiroshima, on August 6, and on Nagasaki, three days later. Further resistance was obviously hopeless, and might even be impossible.

The Surrender of Japan

ACCORDINGLY, on August 10, the Japanese government sued for peace, and Japanese armed forces laid down their arms on August 15. On September 2, representatives of the Japanese government officially surrendered on the deck of the mighty battleship USS *Missouri*, in the waters of Tokyo Bay.

World War II was over. It was won by the combined efforts of soldiers, sailors, and airmen of all of the Allied nations.

But the sailors must have one final word. The war against Japan was fought across a wide ocean. The victory was one of sea power, with the American Navy leading the way.

Index

Iwo Jima, 33, 65-67

Japanese Combined Fleet, 4
Japanese losses, 61
Java Sea, Battle of the, 2
Joint Chiefs of Staff, 41, 43, 44

Kako (Japanese cruiser), 77
Kamikaze tactics, 59, 62, 63, 71, 72, 85
Kerama Islands, 69
King, Ernest J., 41
Kinkaid, Thomas C., 17, 22, 54, 55, 58, 60, 62
Kiska, 22, 23
Koga, Mineichi, 12, 14, 28, 30
Kolombangara, Battle of, 12, 13
Kongo (Japanese battleship), 81
Krueger, Walter, 18, 48
Kula Gulf, Battle of, 12
Kurile Islands, 22
Kurita, Takeo, 14, 35, 51, 52, 53, 56, 58, 61
Kwajalein Atoll, 28
Kyushu, 83

Lae, Papua, 17, 19
Leahey, William D., 42
Lexington (U.S. carrier), 3
Leyte, 42, 43, 44, 48, 62
Leyte Gulf, 52
Lingayan Gulf, 64
Liscome Bay (U.S. carrier), 78
Logistic Support Group, 27
Long Lance torpedoes, 74
Luzon, 42, 62-64

MacArthur, Douglas, 2, 11, 20, 40-42, 83
Makin, 24, 78
Malaya, 2
Marcus Island, 31
Mariana Islands, 30, 33, 40, 65
Marianas Turkey-Shoot, 37
Marines, U.S., 27
Marshall, George C., 41
Marshall Islands, 28

McCain, John S., 52, 54, 59, 60
McMorris, Charles H., 22
Merrill, A. Stanton, 14
Midget submarines, 75
Midway, Battle of, 4, 5
  submarines, 76
Mindanao, 30, 42
Mindoro, 62
Missouri (U.S. battleship), 86
Mitscher, Marc A., 27, 35, 36, 38, 43, 60, 67
Mobile Force (Japan), 51
Morotai, 43
Mogami (Japanese cruiser), 55
Musashi (Japanese battleship), 53

Nautilus (U.S. submarine), 76
Netherlands East Indies, 2
New Guinea, 3, 17, 20, 40
Nimitz, Charles W., 3, 11, 20, 24, 26, 41-44, 48, 60, 83
Nishimura, Shoji, 51, 52, 54

Okinawa, 46, 68
Oldendorf, J.B., 48, 52, 55
Omori, Sentaro, 14
Ozawa, Jisaburo, 32, 33, 34, 51, 54, 58, 60

Pacific Fleet, American, 1
Palau Islands, 30, 42, 43, 80
Papua, 7, 17, 18
Pearl Harbor, 1
Peleliu, 43
Philippines, 41
Philippine Sea, Battle of the, 32-35
Ponape, 28
Port Moresby, 3, 7
Prince of Wales (British battleship), 2
Princeton (U.S. carrier), 54
PT-boats, 55

Rabaul, 11, 19
Radar, 74
Redfin (U.S. submarine), 81

88